FIFTH-CENTURY
ATHENS
DEMOCRACY & CITY STATE

ARTS: A SECOND LEVEL COURSE

The Open
University

BLOCK 4

TENSIONS AND CHANGE IN FIFTH-CENTURY ATHENS

**PREPARED FOR THE COURSE TEAM BY
LORNA HARDWICK AND COLIN CUNNINGHAM**

THE OPEN UNIVERSITY

The Open University

Walton Hall, Milton Keynes MK7 6AA

First published 1996

Edited, designed and typeset by The Open University.

Printed in The United Kingdom by Page Bros (Norwich) Ltd.

ISBN 0 7492 1180 6

This text is a component of the Open University course A209 *Fifth-century Athens: Democracy and City State*. Details of this and other Open University courses are available from Course Enquiries Data Service, PO Box 625, Dane Rd, Milton Keynes MK1 1TY; telephone: + 44 - (0)1908 858585.

a209b4i1.1

CONTENTS

Sections 1 and 4 were written by Lorna Hardwick; Sections 2 and 3 were written by Colin Cunningham; Part 2 (Sections 5–8) were written by Lorna Hardwick.

Colin Cunningham would like to express gratitude to Professor C.M. Robertson for advice and encouragement in the early stages, to Dr Evi Touloupa and Dr Evangelos Kakavoyannis of the Greek Archaeological Service, and to staff of the Greek and Roman Department and the Department of Coins and Medals in the British Museum for advice in the preparation of this block and the associated study material.

STUDY GUIDE FOR BLOCK 4

We have allocated eight weeks for Block 4. Your work on this block is interdisciplinary and integrative: you will at various stages refer to *WA*, the Supplementary Texts, both Illustration Booklets, the Course Guide maps, the TV and Audio-cassette Notes, The Offprints and several of the set books. You will therefore find a note at the beginning of each *section* indicating which parts of the course material are needed when you study it. As a rough guide, you could divide your time like this:

Week 1*   Introduction to Block 4

            Cassette 2, Band 3, 'Gaps in the evidence'

            Cassette 2, Band 4, 'Aristophanes' *The Clouds*: an extract'

            Cassette 3, Band 1, 'The comedies of Aristophanes as a source for social history'

            Preliminary reading of Aristophanes' *The Clouds*
            (optional at this stage)

            TV4, 'Silver – a source of power for the state?
            The evidence of archaeology'

Part 1 The physical and material environment

Week 2   Section 2, including Cassette 3, Band 2, 'Material evidence I: architecture'

Week 3   Section 3, including Cassette 3, Band 3, 'Material evidence II: vase painting'

Week 4   Section 4

Part 2 The Athenian ethos – how the Athenians saw themselves in relation to their environment; how they perceived, interpreted and debated this relationship

Week 5*   Section 5, including TV5, 'Acropolis now ... the public face of the state?'

Week 6   Section 6

Week 7   Section 7, including Cassette 10, Band 1, 'Lecture 3: State and individual in Athens 508–450 BC'

Week 8   Section 8, including Cassette 3 Band 4, 'An introduction to Euripides' *The Women of Troy*'

* with less set reading in these weeks, you have more scope to adjust your study plan, get ahead, or do some further reading.

Sections 7 and 8 contain quite a lot of set reading. You may therefore like to get ahead with your reading of Plato's *Crito* (for Section 7.2) and Euripides' *The Women of Troy* (for Section 8).

INTRODUCTION TO BLOCK 4

1 THE STUDY OF CHANGE

1.1 What do we understand by 'change'?

At the end of the previous block we looked at the passage in which Thucydides (3.82–3) maps out the breakdown in social and political stability and values, which he claims accompanied the intensification of the Peloponnesian War. The examples to which he refers took place in the final quarter of the century we are studying. Nevertheless, the inter-relationship which he describes between events, institutions, beliefs and language assumes the previous existence, in more stable times, of a coherent balance between them.

Clearly Thucydides' outburst raises many questions about the nature, causes, direction and effects of change in general – as well as about the validity of the particular analysis of events which he offers. In this block and the next we are going to investigate some of these questions by exploring certain key themes and looking in detail at some of the major texts and material sources. By the time you get to the Revision Block, Block 6, you should be able both to assess Thucydides' claims more critically and to formulate your own judgements about the pace and direction of change during the century as a whole. You should also be able to identify and discuss some of the underlying causes.

In this short introductory section you will not be asked to do any external reading, apart from that for the cassette exercises at the end of the section. What *is* important is that you think very carefully about what the study of change might entail, and that you formulate a plan for recording your own notes as a commentary on the material you study in Blocks 4 and 5 (suggestions are given in the study guide for Section 4). Then when you get to the Revision Block you will be able to assess the distinctive contribution of the individual themes and sources, and relate them to more general questions. We are not at this stage going to consider the more theoretical aspects of the study of change; but at the end of the course (in the Revision Block) you will be asked to consider examples of modern theories of change and to judge the extent, if any, to which they are of use to historians of the ancient world.

I want to start by asking you to take a common-sense look at our own assumptions about change.

> What do we mean when we talk about 'change'?
> What words do we use to describe it?
> Do we think about change in the abstract, or about changes in things which affect our daily lives?
> What things are important to us in this respect?
> Do we recognize changes as they occur, or afterwards?

Please think about these questions carefully before you read further.

Discussion _____

There is an enormous variety of ways in which we can characterize change. In one sense, the passing of time from day to night and on to another day involves change. Nothing stays the same. We expect that, so we do not remark on it but save the word 'change' for things that alter to such an extent that we have to evolve new ways of coping with them. These can be relatively trivial, such as changes in the weather, or important, like changes in our homes, schools, jobs and government. So already we are talking about chang*es*. But as soon as we respond to one change, we have to fit it in with other aspects of our lives – and sometimes that causes problems. These problems and our resolution of them are reflected in the ways in which we speak about changes – 'planned', 'unexpected', 'disastrous', 'challenging', 'crucial', 'predictable', 'inevitable', 'beneficial', 'progressive', 'temporary', 'permanent', 'far-reaching', etc. All these words (and no doubt you have thought of many more) mark ways in which we *identify* change (usually in retrospect*), classify* it, *analyse* the reasons for it and *evaluate* it. Thus for Thucydides to speak of a 'crisis' or 'collapse' in Greek society involves him in all these activities.

It is useful also to think of what we might regard as the opposite of change – stability? stalemate? continuity? a static situation? tension (balance or equilibrium between potentially opposing factors)? – and note the title to the block!

You might also have mentioned the range of attitudes we adopt to change. We may welcome it if it brings about a state of affairs we want. But often we react against change, especially if it is sudden or unexpected or appears to devalue us as individuals, or as groups. The psychological effects of change may be long-term, affecting our attitude to other aspects of our lives. Sometimes, too, our attitude to a particular change alters over time – for example, a job change may seem good at the time but disastrous in retrospect (or the other way round). Our attitudes may be individual or collective, and may be a response to what we *think* or *believe* has happened as well as to our direct experiences. ◆

1.2   How can we study change in a society?

I started by asking how we as individuals perceive and cope with change. But in this course we are studying Athenian society. What problems might we have in trying to make judgements about *social* change?

Discussion

We would have to consider carefully how we balance evidence about individuals with judgements about the nature and extent of changes affecting society as a whole. The relative lack of evidence about the detailed experiences of individuals perhaps pushes us in the direction of considering larger groups and whole communities.

I think the three most obvious areas we could use for studying changes in Athenian *society* are:

1   *Institutions* (such as the Assembly, the Courts, festivals, organization of the armed forces). We would need to consider *whether* they changed and, if so, *how*. Then we could try to find out why. All this would involve considering changes in the features of an institution itself *and* in its relationship with other institutions and aspects of society. We would need to distinguish between piecemeal changes and structural ones, and between temporary and permanent change.

2   *The broader social and economic framework*, which follows from a study of institutions. So we would need to look for evidence of continuity or change in the legal and social status of different groups (citizens, foreigners, women, slaves etc.), in the sources of wealth and the use to which it was put, in the kind of education or training thought desirable and so on. Such topics very quickly lead into ...

3   *Attitudes and values:* these would include political debate and religious beliefs as well as Athenian assumptions about what was thought desirable or praiseworthy or to be feared. The range of material which could be

included under this heading is enormous. In his book *The Common People* (Fontana, 1984), J.C. Harrison has usefully distinguished between different layers/types of attitude and belief:

i)   beliefs and attitudes which reflect a world-view or set of assumptions about cosmic questions such as the nature and purpose of life and of knowledge. We tend not to spend much time in ordinary life thinking of such matters and, when our assumptions are challenged by philosophers and scientists, the effect can be shattering. An example would be the effect of Darwin's theory on fundamentalist belief that the creation story set out in Genesis is literally true.

ii) beliefs and attitudes which give a framework to the organization of our lives. Examples include political and moral attitudes as reflected in social conventions, legal enactment etc. Such matters are commonly the subject of debate, but underlying pressures for change tend to be slow to be reflected in a new framework. (As examples in our own century, we might cite changes in the laws on homosexuality or divorce.) Where change is dramatic and/or sudden, people tend to be disoriented.

iii) beliefs and attitudes reflected in aspects of life such as taste in art, use of space, design in art and architecture, arrangement of surroundings etc. Change may be slow to percolate to those who are not innovators, and these features may provide a useful index to the *speed* and *extent* of change.

Of course, these three areas tend to shade into one another. Block 4 will tend to concentrate on (ii) and (iii), Block 5 on (i). Taken together they enable us to approach the mental structures, implicit and explicit, within which and sometimes at the bounds of which the Athenians lived, thought and felt.

4   To the above I'd want to add study of the physical environment – land, buildings, food, what people saw or experienced (or expected to) in the course of their daily lives. ◆

At this point please note down anything else which had occurred to you but which I have not mentioned, with the reasons why you think it is important. Then think about whether you see any difficulties in studying change in the way I have suggested.

Discussion

1   A main difficulty arises from the nature of the sources

Quite apart from the accidents of survival, most of the evidence we have was not produced with the intention of helping us answer questions about change. We have very little of the kind of statistical evidence which could be used for comparative analysis, for example. We have no mass observation to help us consider popular attitudes in the ancient world. We have a few written sources which give an individual response to change, but they are virtually all written from the viewpoint of the privileged classes. To escape from the strait-jacket of these sources, we have first to give careful thought to the way we can use non-literary evidence (for example, buildings, inscriptions, iconography etc.). Secondly, we have to confront the special problems of studying changes and developments in attitudes and thought-patterns and structures. As part of this activity we need to consider whether there are ways of studying the lives and attitudes of the ordinary people who do not speak directly as individuals through the sources. Are there ways in which we can identify their collective role in the society we are studying? What would be the consequences of failure to tackle this dimension?

Figure 1 Attic 'bilingual' amphora, provenance unknown. Herakles and the Cretan bull by the Andokides painter (red figure) and the Lysippides painter (black figure), *c*.525 (height 20.75in., 53.25cm.) (Cat.99.538; ARV 4.12). The exploits of the mythical and heroic characters were part of the mental 'framework of reference' familiar to all Athenians.

2 Time-span

Whether we identify changes and how we account for them depends to a large extent on *when* we look (as well as where). So we have to distinguish between short-term changes and lasting changes, *and* between relatively sudden, acute changes and those which can only be identified over a substantial span of time.

For example, we have taken the fifth century as the 'period' for our course. Yet a substantial body of academic opinion would say that there is important continuity between Archaic art and society (seventh and sixth centuries) and early classical (first half of the fifth century). So to what extent do we look back earlier than the beginning of the fifth century in order to assess changes? What do we take as our yardstick?

Another example occurs at the end of the fifth century. Our assessment of the impact of the Athenian defeat will depend on whether we compare the last years of the century *only* with the prosperity and confidence of the mid-century, or whether we look at a longer perspective and see what happened afterwards in the fourth century (this is one reason for the stress on Plato's work in Section 7 and in Block 5). It is fair to say that in any assessment of change, we have to try to identify a key point and then look *before* and *afterwards*, but it is a matter of argument about how *far* we need to go on any particular issue. ◆

In both parts of the block we have selected examples of texts, buildings and art forms which will yield significant evidence relevant to the study of change. But we have also selected them because they are exciting and enjoyable to study in their own right.

1.3   Audio-cassette tutorials

There are three cassette tutorials associated with this part of the block. **It is important that you work on these now, in order, before reading further in the block.**

1.4   Cassette 2, Band 3: 'Gaps in the evidence'

You will need to listen to this carefully and work through the exercises contained in the Audio-cassette Notes. The cassette examines possible approaches to the problems of method identified in this section and explores some of the ways in which we can try to overcome the problems of the gaps in the evidence available to us. We will focus especially on possible ways of identifying and analysing collective attitudes.

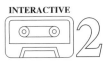

1.5   Cassette 2, Band 4: 'Aristophanes' *The Clouds*: an extract'

This cassette band provides an introduction to *The Clouds* as performance. Listen to it now.

1.6   Cassette 3, Band 1: 'The comedies of Aristophanes as a source for social history'

This cassette tutorial follows on from the previous two, and *it is essential to study it at this point*. It also provides a way in to your study of Aristophanes. If you have time, you may like to read the whole play before going any further.

PART 1   THE PHYSICAL AND MATERIAL ENVIRONMENT

Study guide for Sections 2 and 3

In approaching Athenian art and architecture and vase painting in these sections of the block, we shall be working at two levels. First, we shall consider the buildings, sculptures and vases as works of art on their own terms. You will be learning the skills needed to study art and architecture rather as you initially approached *Prometheus Bound* and *Antigone* as dramas. The cassette tutorials are designed to teach you the conventions and give you practice in the necessary skills, and the Illustration Booklets will enable you to look closely at a wide range of examples.

Secondly, you will be asked to begin to relate your detailed work on art and architecture to the overall themes of the block, and to use them to begin to identify areas of tension and change in fifth-century Athens. Material evidence certainly helps us to identify features of continuity or permanence in the physical environment. Public buildings and public art may be interpreted as expressions of collective decisions about magnificence, the use of space, and rituals, and so may help us to understand collective experience and attitudes. Both private art and public art help us to identify trends and developments in taste and surroundings.

Initially the first level of study will take most of your time and energy. But we suggest you pause at the end of Section 2 and again at the end of Section 3 to relate what you have studied to the overall themes of the block. You may find it helpful to focus your study of each section by keeping in mind three guiding questions and making short notes on these at the end of each section:

1   What is the contribution of the sources in this section to a study of the material environment of the Athenians?

2   Can we use evidence gleaned from these sources to approach other aspects of Athenian life and attitudes?

3   How does this evidence help us to study change in the fifth century? What kind of change/changes are we meeting? Does any of the evidence point to continuity and stability rather than change?

For this and the following section you will need to have by you the following items:

The World of Athens
Texts
Illustration Booklets I and II
TV and Audio-cassette Illustration Booklet
The Offprints

The printed text and the cassette bands will refer you to illustrations in all three booklets because there is, obviously, no absolute distinction between the items illustrated. We have availed ourselves of the limited amount of better quality paper in the Illustration Booklets to print most of the photographs there: we hope this will give you a better standard of reproduction. The use of different booklets should also make some of the comparisons easier to make. However, the principal divisions are as follows:

Illustration Booklet I: photographs of architecture and sculpture for study in Section 2.

Illustration Booklet II: colour plates for the whole of Block 4 and photographs of vase paintings for study with Section 3.

TV and Audio-cassette Illustration Booklet: illustrations for cassette exercises, as well as for use with television programmes.

In this block: diagrams for in-text exercises in Part 4.

Illustrations in the Illustration Booklets are referred to as Plate I.1, I.2 etc. for Illustration Booklet I, and II.1, II.2 etc. for Illustration Booklet II. Illustrations in the TV and Audio-cassette Illustrations are referred to as Plate 1, Plate 2 etc. Illustrations in the block are referred to as Figure 1, Figure 2 etc. This should become clear as you work through the material.

In addition to the printed illustrations, TV5 is closely integrated with this block and relates to your study of the Periclean Acropolis in Section 2.3.

2 ATHENIAN ART AND ARCHITECTURE

2.1 Introduction

A course on fifth-century Athens without a study of the buildings of the Acropolis would be seriously deficient. However, it is no easy matter to interpret these buildings and their sculpture. They have acquired the status of great monuments in the development of Western culture, and have been taken as standards of beauty and excellence since the late eighteenth century (see Figure 2). There are scarcely any written fifth-century references to them, so we cannot be sure how they were appreciated by Athenians or by other Greeks of our period. We have, however, chosen to include a section on Athenian art and architecture in this block on the study of change – because the study of non-literary evidence of this sort should prompt new types of question about the nature of change in Athenian society. But there is also the reverse argument, that your opinions about the nature and causes of change may help to focus your interpretation of these 'great monuments'.

The rebuilding of the Acropolis is referred to at three main points in *WA* – as part of the physical environment (1.34), as the background to religious activity (2.38–49) and as part of the intellectual world (7.75–8). Sections 7.64–5 are also relevant.

Read these pages quickly now and consider whether any of them adequately explain the temples and sculptures.

Discussion ────────────────────────────

Obviously, the separate sections of *WA* are adequate, taken individually. It is possible to see works of the classical period as a stage in the development of Greek sculpture (7.75–6); but that raises the question of the place of art in Greek society (7.64–5). Since we are talking about temples and temple sculpture, their religious function is clearly important, and 2.40 makes the point that both civic and sacred functions were under the patronage of the gods. Finally 1.34 links the development to the political position of Athens as victor in the Persian Wars. Even so, I doubt if you felt in much of a position to assess the art and architecture of Periclean Athens; though the fact that so much survives from the Acropolis makes that group of buildings important. ◆

Figure 2 A view of the Acropolis in the late eighteenth century. The French consul is being served by his Turkish servant, surrounded by the sculptured fragments he was collecting. Note the metope from the Parthenon, which is now in the British Museum. This picture is a reminder of the way British and other collectors set about acquiring Greek works of art. As a result of their efforts, Greek sculpture and architecture became known in the West and came to be regarded as key monuments of Western civilization.

I think our task is threefold. First we need to work out what each temple or sculpture was, and how it worked. (Much of your study of this will be based on cassette exercises.) Then we need to consider how the various temples and sculptures fitted into the fifth century. Only then can we begin to ask questions about interpretation.

2.2   The problem of ruins

> Suppose ... that the city of Sparta were to become deserted, and that only the temples and foundations of buildings remained, I think that future generations would ... find it very difficult to believe that the place had really been as powerful as it was represented to be. ... If, on the other hand, the same thing were to happen to Athens, one would conjecture from what met the eye that the city had been twice as powerful as in fact it is.

> (Thucydides, 1.10)

Thucydides' contemporary warning is a salutary reminder of the need to be careful in assessing unwritten evidence. But the fact that he makes the comment at all suggests a recognition of the important part played by public building in any *polis*. The problem is, by what standards do we judge such things? Figure 2 above, and Plates I.1–4, I.7–9 and I.90 in Illustration Booklet I show some of the difficulties. First, the art of Classical Athens has been admired and collected by other nations since the eighteenth century. Second, we tend to have a romanticized view of these buildings simply because they are ruins; and our enjoyment of sites such as Sounion may have as much to do with Byron as with fifth-century Athens.

Mountains look on Marathon, and Marathon looks on the sea.
And, dreaming there an hour alone, I dreamed that Greece might
still be free.

(Byron, *Don Juan*, III, 86, 3)

This attitude may help to explain *our* interest in fifth-century Athens, but does
not explain fifth-century Athens itself. We need to set the buildings in context.
Here Plate I.3 is some improvement on Plate I.1 because there are more
remains, and we can see the temples in relation to one another. But we also
need to discover what they were like in the fifth century, and how they
worked. TV5 explores this theme; and a comparison of the two pictures in
Plate I.90 helps. Yet there are still difficulties of dating and reconstruction, for
which we rely on archaeologists. But before discussing the Acropolis, we need
to look at temple buildings as examples of the public material evidence of fifth-
century Athens. Only then can we begin to use that evidence, alongside the
other sources we have, to answer our questions about tensions and change,
relationships between individuals, institutions and the state, and so on.

Figure 3 Reconstructed drawings (with plans) of model
temples dedicated as votive offerings. Left, from the Argive
Heraeum; right, from Perachora. Eighth century BCE.

However, it is difficult, and even unwise, to study only fifth-century Attic temples. Their relationship to earlier (and later) buildings is important. And it is
quite clear that architecture and sculpture were not confined by the borders of
any *polis*. Pheidias, the sculptor of the Parthenon, produced his greatest work in
the statue of Zeus at Olympia. Iktinos, the architect of the Parthenon, went on to
build the temple of Apollo at Bassae in the Peloponnese (Plate I.14) for the
Phigeleans (whose troops had fought alongside the Athenians). It is quite possible that the unfinished temple at Segesta (or Egesta) in Sicily (see the plan in
Plate 13 in the TV and Audio-cassette Illustration Booklet, and Thucydides 6.6)
was designed by an Athenian; and it has even been suggested that the sculptors
who worked on the Parthenon frieze may previously have been employed by
the Persian King at Persepolis.

Such details may raise interesting historical speculations; but what is important
is that public art and architecture on the scale of the Periclean Acropolis always
had an importance that went far beyond the *polis* of Attica itself. So our interpretation of the public architecture of Athens must take account of her position
(economic and political) in the ancient world. Thucydides pointed out the effects of such display, and we may assume that Pericles was equally aware of
the possibilities. But clearly the impact of rebuilt sanctuaries would be judged
by comparison with temples and sanctuaries elsewhere. So we must now look
at temple buildings in general.

INTERACTIVE

Turn now to Cassette 3, Band 2: 'Material evidence I: architecture'.

2.3 The Periclean Acropolis

We can now continue our study with an analysis of some of the buildings of the Acropolis and their function.

Turn to the plan of the Acropolis (Plate 14 in the TV and Audio-cassette Illustration Booklet) and answer the following:

1 *How many buildings can you make out on the Acropolis?*

2 *How many of the buildings are temples?*

Discussion _____

This isn't as easy as it seems. I make the total eleven; but you may well differ unless, like me, you simply counted the buildings as they are listed in the key. For instance, I have counted the sanctuary of Artemis Brauronia as one; but, as it is laid out around three sides of a court, you might argue that it was three buildings, or even four. And, since there is a passage linking it to the colonnade of the Chalkotheke, which shares a wall with it, you could claim the two complexes were one. Here again, we are relying on archaeological evidence, which distinguishes the different structures mentioned as being on the Acropolis (in inscriptions and later descriptions such as that by Pausanias in the second century CE). Then again, did you count the temple of Athene Nike as on the Acropolis or not? The worship of Athene Nike (Athene, goddess of Victory) was ancient on this site, and the fifth-century temple merely a new shrine; but although it is on the hilltop (Plate I.3), it stands outside the wall and gateway. If you find this surprising, remember that the Acropolis was also an ancient fortress, whose walls were laid out for defence. And, of course, the Acropolis was not the only religious site in Athens.

My second question is a little easier, but still not entirely simple. Six buildings – the temple of Athene Nike, the shrine of Artemis Brauronia, the Parthenon, the Precinct of Pandion, the Precinct of Zeus Polieus and the Erechtheion – were buildings for some form of worship. But not all of these are temple buildings (and the big altar of Athene is left out). In fact, we can agree that the temple of Athene Nike and the Erechtheion are temples; and, of course, there is the Parthenon. But, if you compare the temple of Athene Nike with the buildings in the Precinct of Zeus and in the Court of the Pandroseion, I think you will agree that they are similar, and the latter can also clearly be classed as small temples. Yet how vastly different from the Parthenon. ◆

One thing, however, is worth remembering. The survival of traditional elements in the architecture and of traditional forms, indeed the firmness of the whole temple tradition, and the effort put into maintaining it, can certainly be seen as an indication of the extent to which Athenian society did not change in the fifth century; or, at least, that forces opposed to change were at work.

It seems to me that this continuity in the plans of temples closely matches the craft tradition of the masons who built them (to which I referred on Cassette 3, Band 2). If you compare Plates I.5–7, you will find it is difficult to detect any major changes in the methods of construction (dry stone, columns made of piles of drums, etc.) or the forms that resulted (size of capital, relation of entablature to column height, etc.). The quality of the Parthenon as an architectural form rests very largely on its accumulation of subtleties (a slight curve in the taper of the columns and in the surface of the stylobate, modifications in the column spacing, etc.), which seem to me to derive from a tradition of masonry which goes back to the eighth century BCE. In that case the architecture shows slow development rather than change, and there is no tension between the earlier and later forms.

You might argue that the plan of the Erechtheion (see Plate 14 in the TV and Audio-cassette Illustration Booklet, and Plates I.12–13 in Illustration Booklet I) indicates a change. Yet there are special reasons for its form, and it was the shrine of the ancient cult statue of Athene Polias, replacing the old temple whose site lay between it and the Parthenon (Plate 14). That is to say that, as a religious site, the Erechtheion has a longer history than the Parthenon, and so could be seen as more traditional.

Two factors seem particularly important here (and they will be discussed further in TV7). First, the buildings suggest a real persistence of traditional forms in religion. Second, the physical shape given to those traditional forms in architecture was the most prestigious form of building in fifth-century Attica. (You will see the remains of some other buildings in TV6 and study private housing in Sections 4.5 and 4.6 of this block.) Further evidence of the importance of this traditional strand of fifth-century Athenian life is in the number of temples built or rebuilt in the period. (Check the dates of Attic temples in TV and Audio-cassette Illustration Booklet, Plate 13, and look at Plates I.1, I.2 and I.8.) The most radical formal change seems to me the new colonnade of the temple of Athene at Sounion (you will see this in more detail in TV7), which partly transforms a much older temple – with a plan harking back to Mycenean times into a conventional classical temple.

If we accept, therefore, that temple buildings represent continuity rather than change, this needs to be set against the clear evidence of development in other fields, from specific economic changes (for example, at Laureion, which you saw in TV4) to social change (see Section 4) or new philosophical ideas (see Block 5).

2.3.1 The Propylaia

The first building you come to on the Acropolis is the Propylaia, or ceremonial gateway, which prepares the way for the Parthenon. You will see how the 'rules' of Doric (which you studied on Cassette 3, Band 2) are subtly broken, and what lengths the architect, Mnesikles, went to in order to achieve his effect. (You may need to refer back to Plate 12 in the TV and Audio-cassette Illustration Booklet to check the names of some of the parts.)

Look carefully at the plans in Plate 14 (TV and Audio-cassette Illustration Booklet) and at Plates I.3, 10, 11, 15–17 and 91 (Illustration Booklet I). Also read the description of the Propylaia by Pausanias (ST 21a). Then make notes on the following questions:

1   *How did the Propylaia function?*

2   *What problems did it pose for its architect?*

3   *Does the building reflect traditional values or not?*

Discussion —————————————————————————————————

The Propylaia was the only entrance to the Acropolis, a great hall with five doorways bridging the sacred road up to the Acropolis. To the north was what Pausanias described as a picture gallery; but its use seems obscure. It seems also – the Propylaia was never fully completed – that there were intended to be two inner halls, possibly as part of the servicing arrangements for the festivals. It is interesting that Pausanias singles out the marble ceiling as outstanding; but that suggests to me that he is thinking of the way the building was experienced. The ceiling would be very visible as you approached up the steep ramp. You would then move out of the daylight into the shadowed hall, pass through one of the gates and then emerge from darkness to light within the sacred enclosure of the Acropolis.

The laying out of a plan as complex as this on such a steeply sloping site is a tribute to the mathematical skills of the architect, Mnesikles. Notice how the courses of the foundation bastion are successively swung through a slight angle (Plate I.15), so that the base of the building is precisely aligned with the top course of the bastion. But the complexity does not stop there. The small columns of the wings stand on the same stylobate as the larger ones of the centre; but the proportion of stylobate to column is maintained by the visual device of cutting it in four steps instead of three, and having the lowest made of grey marble on the wings so that only the three white steps are read as stylobate. (This can be seen in Plate I.11.) Inside, the slope of the hill meant that only one step of stylobate was possible (see Plate I.10) – a departure from the norm, but one that would hardly be noticed, as your attention would be on the Parthenon and other shrines ahead.

There are invisible ingenuities in the splendid ceiling. It was, in fact, supported on iron beams concealed within the marble. Plain stone would not have sufficient bearing strength. Also, the architect has mixed the orders. The columns of the hall are Ionic, for a very good reason. Because the columns of the Ionic order are taller and slimmer – for a given diameter – than Doric, these were tall enough to support the ceiling (which rests above the Doric frieze), but need be no wider than the Doric columns of the facade, which thus conceal them (see Plate I.16). All this is extremely sophisticated, and indicates the skill of both Mnesikles and his masons.

How, then, do we interpret such a building? Is it a unique 'monument of genius'? Does it represent a development, or does it mainly reinforce tradition?

Architects of the last hundred years have generally agreed that the Propylaia is an outstanding building, and it is certainly unique. But that qualitative assessment says more about the interest of architects in the classical roots of Western culture than it reveals about the way its builders perceived the Propylaia. Surely for them its significance and quality lay in its relation to the other monuments of the Acropolis? It matches the style of the Parthenon (which also uses Ionic columns in its *opisthodomos*, or rear room, see Figure 4), and uses many identical mouldings. They were probably cut by the very same masons, using the same templates. Yet it contrasts with the shrine itself by being completely devoid of sculpture. In all these senses it is well fitted to its purpose as the gateway to the sacred *temenos* (or sanctuary); and this shows great *techne*. It is more elaborate than any earlier gateway that we know; and so presumably demonstrates the power and wealth of Athens as well as a stage in the development of building. Yet it is designed within the traditional forms of the Doric order (in spite of the difficulties). And did you notice that it overlies the Kimonian gate quite precisely? The traditional position of the entry to the *temenos* is carefully maintained. ◆

This section has, I hope, shown you some of the skills needed to analyse this type of evidence, and also the difficulties of interpreting the works. I want now to use these skills and face the difficulties of interpretation in relation to the grandest building of the Acropolis – the Parthenon.

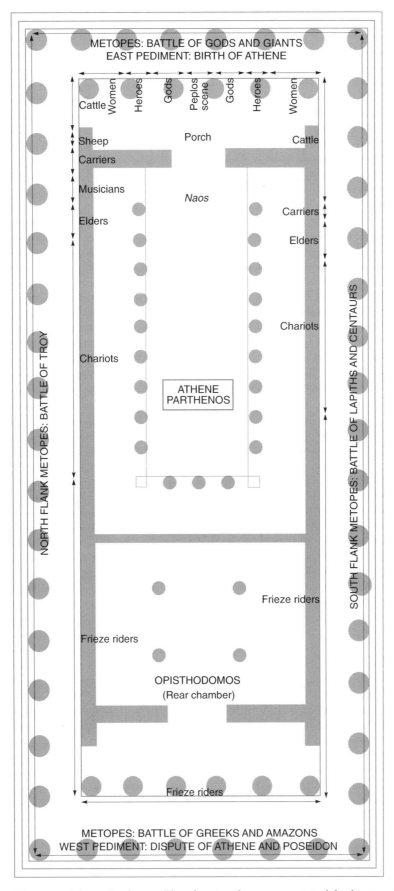

Figure 4 Athens: Parthenon. Plan showing the arrangement of the frieze and the metopes.

2.3.2 The Parthenon

The Parthenon is the principal temple and the largest building on the Acropolis. You will see more of this building in TV5; but, for the present, I want you to focus your study on three questions:

1   What was it, and how did it function?

2   What makes the building so special architecturally?

3   How do the sources we have allow us to interpret it?

Begin by looking at Figure 4, in conjunction with Plate 14, 23c and 24 (TV and Audio-cassette Illustration Booklet), and Plates I.3–4 and I.7–9. (You may also like to look at the sculpture, Plates I.19–34 and 51–55, though that will be discussed later.)

Read the descriptions by Plutarch (ST 24b) and Pausanias (ST 21b), and check WA 1.34, 2.38–9, 2.49 and 7.78. Then make notes in answer to my questions.

Discussion _____

Three things stand out. First, the Parthenon is only part of a larger development that included the Propylaia, the Erechtheion and the temple of Athene Nike. Secondly, the whole development can be seen as the public statement of Athens' recovery from the Persian sack of 490, and her position as an imperial power (especially since the development was paid for out of tribute money). Finally, in this series of shrines for the principal civic religion, the Parthenon was not the home of the most sacred image. That was in the Erechtheion (Plate I.12–13) built in the contrasting Ionic style with much rich and delicate ornament. It is important to remember that the *temenos* (or sanctuary) was as important as the individual shrine, and the bulk of the Acropolis is covered by a series of linked *temenoi* of Athene. The Parthenon is merely the largest and most elaborate of the shrines. You may also have noticed the unusual plan with a completely separate room, the *opisthodomos*, to the west. This was used to house the state treasury, and so links the building very closely with Athens' imperial position.

Still, the Parthenon was more than just a treasury. The bulk of the interior space was given over to a colossal gold and ivory statue of the goddess, over 12 metres high (see Plate I.25). The layout of the *naos*, with its internal colonnade, two tiers of Doric columns running right round the statue (and a shallow pool in front of it for reflected light), is even more elaborate than the great temple of Zeus at Olympia. As a building, the Parthenon has long been famous for the extraordinary, almost imperceptible subtlety of its stonework; and the architect, Iktinos, is known to have published a treatise on the building that presumably detailed this. The stylobate is curved upwards, a mere ten centimetres on the whole length of 70 metres. The sides of the columns taper along a subtle curve; and their axes are adjusted so that the columns lean very slightly inwards (Plates I.7, 8 and 90). Did you spot it? If not, check again.

Scholars still argue whether the purpose of these refinements was optical correction or exaggeration, or even whether they have a symbolic value. Whatever the reason, it seems to me that their mere achievement suggests a long and well-established tradition of masonry. And here it is perhaps worth remembering that the Greeks had no word for art except *techne*, which also includes what we mean by craft and skill. This is important, for over the last two centuries the Parthenon has all too often been seen as the culminating aesthetic achievement of ancient Greece, more famous for the sculptures (which we shall discuss in the next section) than anything else.

Finally, notice that Plutarch is impressed with the speed of the whole enterprise. We know from inscriptions that the Parthenon took about fifteen years to build:

447–439: construction of temple, fitting of carved metopes, making of ceilings and roof, carving of frieze.

442–438: work on chryselephantine (gold and ivory) statue of the goddess.

438: dedication of the statue at the Great Panathenaia.

440–432: work on the pediment sculptures.

This is certainly impressive, though it probably seemed swifter to Plutarch writing 700 years later than to any young Athenian watching the building grow year by year. I am impressed by the technological achievement – some 22,000 tons of marble quarried from Mount Pentelikon, and transported 16 kilometres to Athens (not to mention marble roof tiles imported from Paros), all raised 120 metres up the Acropolis hill, and then carved and shaped with great precision and subtlety. The list of craftsmen cited by Plutarch is a useful reminder of the extent to which work on the temple of the Acropolis affected the life of Athens.

However, our written sources are problematic. Plutarch and Pausanias offer the most detailed ancient descriptions we have; but neither is contemporary, so their assessments need treating with caution. The first thing to notice is that neither author seems much interested in the architecture as such. By their time, the sophisticated development of hallowed traditions seemed unimportant, and the high level of *techne* was ignored. Pausanias, writing in the second century CE for Roman philhellenes, has an antiquarian interest in the myths and dedications. He is impressed with the cult statue and the pediments, but does not even mention the frieze which – because of its survival – may seem more important to us.

Plutarch's view, with its stress on economics, reads more persuasively. However, it is important to remember that his references to the Parthenon are merely elements in his portrayal of Pericles as a great leader. We cannot necessarily read them as the standard reaction, still less as representative of fifth-century Athens. When you study the Funeral Oration in Section 5 of this block, you should consider whether the attitudes expressed there are parallel to Plutarch's. I believe there is a considerable degree of overlap, and that we can see the Periclean Acropolis as a conscious programme of display. However, the most important factor in my mind is the historical situation. The Parthenon was built before the outbreak of the Peloponnesian War, but is an integral part of the whole Acropolis development – which was not completed until almost the end of the war. I think we can infer from this that the prestige, even the identity, of the *polis* was intimately involved in the completion of the entire project. The Parthenon, the grandest part, was merely completed first. ◆

2.3.3 The sculptures of the Parthenon

Because the Parthenon, like other ancient temples, is ruined and its sculptures scattered in museums, it is very difficult to see them as other than museum pieces. In this sub-section, I shall be discussing the interpretation of the sculptures and considering the part they played in fifth-century Athens. In each case it is important to try to establish the proper context, so we have provided standard captions to help. These give the original location, description, material and size (where known) and the present location of each piece. Every time you study a plate you should identify the original location, using Figures 4–9. Scale is also difficult to recover. Compare for instance the impact of the sculptures as shown in Plates I.80a and I.80c. Each time you study a plate you should check the size mentally against something in your own room. Material is also important. Compare, for instance, II.IV and II.V with I.77 and I.79. The comparison of I.71 with II.VI also reminds you of the difference between coloured and black and white reproduction. The sculptures of the Parthenon are all of marble, though there were bronze attachments and they may well have been coloured (compare II.III with I.70). Certainly the backgrounds of metopes and frieze were coloured. Compare the effect of I.55 and Figure 6. It requires a conscious effort to bear all these points in mind when you study reproductions of the sculpture in your own room.

Figure 5 Athens: Parthenon. Drawing showing location of sculptures (after G. Niemann).

There seem to me to be three main ways of interpreting the Parthenon and its sculptures.

a) as state propaganda

b) as the product of religious fervour

c) as an aesthetic experience

Figure 6 Athens: Parthenon. North frieze. Drawing of slabs XXXVI–XXXVIII from the North frieze to show the effect of the blue background. Compare plate I.55.

It is, of course, difficult to separate these views; but we need to consider them before deciding which one(s) help most in studying the development of fifth-century Athens.

Figure 7 Athens: Parthenon. West pediment drawn by Jacques Carrey, 1674.

So, look at the sculptures (Plates I.19–34 and I.51–55), and at Figures 4–9. Re-read Pausanias (ST 21b) and Plutarch (ST 24b) and read WA 7.64–76. Then make notes on what aspects of the Parthenon sculptures could be cited as evidence for each of my three views. (You will probably find it useful to spend some time checking each plate against Figures 4 and 7–9, to see exactly where on the building each sculpture was set.)

Discussion

For the propagandist view, I would cite the martial image of the maiden goddess, both inside the temple and on the pediments (in the story of her birth she sprang fully armed from the head of Zeus). The statue of the Parthenos is also related to the image of Athene Promachos (see TV and Audio-cassette Illustration Booklet, Plate 14, and Plate I.91), a 9-metre-high bronze statue also by Pheidias. Fragments of the base of this suggest a date around 460 (other scholars argue for a date about 465, under Kimon), when it was dedicated 'from the spoils of the Persians'. The scenes of the metopes all illustrate famous mythical conflicts between barbarism and civilization (in which the forces of civilization triumphed). Then there is the frieze which illustrated a part of the Panathenaic procession in honour of Athene. This stress on the goddess in external sculpture is unusual in Greek temples. There is also the sheer extent of the decoration, something that was never achieved again in mainland Greece. This was the first temple to have all the metopes carved (the temple of Zeus at Olympia (Plate I.36) only had carved metopes in the entrance porch). The encircling frieze, 160 metres long, is unique. And we have already discussed the special qualities of the building. All these elements could have a propagandist purpose; and it is surely relevant that the major festival of the Acropolis, the Panathenaia, involved the allies – as well as the Athenians – in sending sacrifices.

There is, then, a strong case for seeing the Periclean Acropolis as propagandist. But can we really distinguish that message and the emotion of a civic religion? The stress on Athene, and on the benefits she gave Attica – the west pediment showing her conflict with Poseidon was a reminder of this, and there were further reminders in the Erechtheion – seems to me equally valid as a religious emotion; and the extent of the decoration could also be the result of religious fervour. The traditional myths were very much alive in the fifth century, and

23

were still the focus of both the new temples and the continuing festivals. (This idea is explored in detail in TV7.) Dramatists such as Euripides can be seen as questioning the literal truth of the myths, though one can also argue that they were using old myths to explore new problems.

We have the same problem in relation to the Parthenon sculptures. Both pediments and frieze relate to the myth of Athene; and the frieze is perhaps the more interesting place to begin. Its continuous strip seems to be a picture of the procession bringing the sacred robe, or *peplos*, to Athene. But it is clearly a selective picture, not a straightforward presentation. It does not, for instance, show the sacred ship, which we know from other sources formed part of the procession. One interpretation suggests that the frieze commemorates the Athenian dead at Marathon, and points out that the number of men equates with the number of Athenian casualties. But if so, we need to cope with the problem of hoplite soldiers portrayed as mounted warriors – that is, as traditional aristocratic fighters. This seems a little odd on a temple erected by a democracy. Of course, there was a problem that mortals had never before been shown on a temple; and the traditions of religious formality might well make it more appropriate to have such commemorative figures heroized in that way. Another view sees the figures as so many images of the ideal citizen. Notice how little the faces are differentiated. This, combined with the way the frieze would be seen, in sections between pillars, suggests that it should be read episodically rather than as a single commemorative procession. Nonetheless both the commemoration of fallen warriors, and the stress on the ideal citizen's involvement with his protectress deity, have to be read as possibly resulting from a religious motive. Besides, the Parthenon is a temple, and its re-use of column drums from the older temple is a further indication of the importance of tradition. It was linked to the other main temple of the *temenos*, the Erechtheion, as the focus of what was probably the grandest Athenian religious festival.

One aspect of Pausanias' description is puzzling. He pays no more attention to the external sculpture than we do to the sculpture on the facade of the British Museum or the average town hall. Pausanias obviously has an antiquarian interest in the Parthenos statue; and, admittedly, he was writing centuries later. However, it is significant that he virtually ignores the largest surviving collection of datable classical sculpture. Perhaps, for him, it was only one of many sets of sculpture, and individual votive statues were better or more highly thought of. At any rate we need to guard against exaggerating the regard for these works at the time. Plate I.7 and Figure 5 show how difficult it must have been to see the frieze. Yet it is also significant how carefully the various images were designed. The background, at least, of frieze and metopes were coloured (Figure 6) so that the images stood out. Did you also notice the depth of relief of the metopes (Plate I.23) and the way the heads are often set close to the top of the slab, so that, from below, they would have stood out strongly, breaking the straight line of the edge of the frieze band? And the compositions are often extremely sophisticated (Plates I.19–22). What is particularly impressive is the sense of unity (compare Plates I.20 and I.21). Obviously the carving involved a large number of different sculptors of differing skill. This can easily be seen by comparing the drapery or the treatment of beards in Plates I.22 and 24. Some of the sculptors evidently found the management of struggling poses quite difficult (Plate I.22); but the overall consistency is so striking that we can accept (and be impressed by) the single guiding mind, that of Pheidias.

The frieze shows even greater uniformity than the metopes, perhaps because the team of sculptors was more used to working together. But there are still differences. Compare the treatment of the horses' manes in Plates I.38, 51 and 55, or the composition of the cavalcade on the south side (Plate I.51) – fairly regular, almost monotonous – and on the north (Plate I.55), which is lively and varied. There is considerable skill in adapting the composition to the long narrow band of the frieze. Look at Plates I.28–31 and I.51–55, and see how figures are shown mounted, standing in chariots or seated (if they are gods, and therefore larger than life size), all within the one-metre height of the frieze. You can see also from examples how the procession moves insistently forward (very few figures look back), and how the rhythm changes – galloping along the sides, but slowly at the approach to the sacred stone over the entrance.

The handling of relief, too, is very skilful. Notice how the horses are shown overlapping; yet nowhere is the relief deeper than two or three inches. Low-relief carving had a long tradition in Greece, so it is less surprising that it is so highly developed on the Parthenon. But it is used alongside the very high relief of the metopes (Plate I.23) and the free-standing figures of the pediments – even their invisible backs are fully carved.

Scholars have reconstructed the composition of the pediments (Figures 8 and 9) but the remains are very fragmentary. Nonetheless they too show great quality. Compare the musculature of Plates I.32 and I.35: the figure from the Parthenon is more lifelike. You can sense the weight that pulls the flesh of the stomach over. There is the same skill in the drapery (also presumably by different sculptors). Plate I.33 shows how the folds are arranged to lie across the form and reveal the roundness of the underlying body. Actually this is a sculptor's trick. Drapery would not naturally fall this way; but we see the shadows and the line of the folds, and read the shapes underneath more clearly. By contrast, the flying Iris (Plate I.34) has a thin material pressed against her body as she rushes through the air. ◆

I have dealt at some length with the aesthetic qualities of the Parthenon sculptures, which were described in 1807 as sufficient to 'at last rouse the art of Europe from its slumber of darkness'. Since then they have been seen by succeeding generations of critics as outstanding works of genius. Yet we see only broken fragments, missing their colour and all their bronze attachments. (Notice the holes for bronze bridles in Plate I.31.) Although they are not part of Pausanias' interest, these issues are important in assessing the sculptures as part of the development of Greek or Western art. They present as much a problem for our interpretation as we find in the attempt to recover an 'authentic' meaning in Greek drama. Certainly our assessment of the Parthenon sculptures as 'great works of art' is not the same as 'reading' them in the way a fifth-century Athenian might. We can however point to aspects that may be important, on the assumption that what was novel would have attracted attention. The size of the temple is important here, and no other temple had been as extensively decorated with sculpture before. This, I think, has implications for the Athenians' view of the grandeur and power of their town. Then the use of the myth of Athene to celebrate the protectress of the city was a novelty. Other temples (for examples, Plates I.36–7) were not exclusively decorated with the myths of the deity to whom they were dedicated. If we include the metopes, the sculptural programme of the Parthenon probably raised an awareness of the special nature and the civilizing mission of Athens. Finally, the frieze with its reference to the traditional forms of worship can be seen to elevate the status of the Athenian citizen by association with his protectress's deity.

2.3.4 Assessment of Greek public art

We can now begin to ask the wider question about how the Parthenon and the Acropolis as a whole fitted into Athenian society. Did the art and architecture serve to reinforce traditional values or help to shape new ones? We might begin by considering who saw these things, and under what circumstances.

The buildings of the Acropolis were, of course, visited by Athenians as well as allies, but I think the presumption is that they were seen mostly on festival days. The Panathenaia was only the grandest of several festivals of Athene, so the average citizen might have seen the temples fairly frequently. The allies would certainly have seen the Acropolis at the Panathenaia, but none of them saw the works as we do.

We can see these sculptures as part of the conspicuous display of the Periclean Acropolis. Plates I.18, 40, 43, 66 and Plate 16 show samples of the sculpture and decoration on other buildings of the Acropolis. This is an indication of the

Figure 8 Athens: Parthenon. West pediment. Composition reconstructed by Prof. E. Berger from casts assembled from different museums.

Figure 9 Athens: Parthenon. East pediment. Composition reconstructed by Prof. E. Berger from casts assembled from different museums.

status of Athens at that time. We can also compare them stylistically with earlier and later work (Plates I.35–6 and I.39–40), and recognize that there is a development in Greek art in which the Parthenon sculptures represent the High Classical Moment. But we are still left with the knowledge that here we are looking at a great expression of state art, and it is difficult to establish what meaning that had for the average Athenian. Even aesthetically the sculptures are not entirely unproblematic.

By way of revision, look closely at all the illustrations of heads, and ask what expression, if any, is shown. ◆

Discussion _____

Although the figures are all quite lifelike, I think it is fairly easy to see that there is not much variety of expression. The faces are all very similar and rather solemn, some say empty-headed. Perhaps that is because this is merely state art, and lacks the personal dimension. If so, we should look at some private art to consider if there is a difference.

2.4 The problem of Greek art

At this point, however, we should pause to reconsider some of the problems of studying Greek art. First of all, you should not underestimate the difficulty of working from fragments, or of seeing pieces in museums rather than in their original position. Can we be really sure, for instance, of the pose of a fragmentary figure (for example, Plate I.34)? How significant is the loss of painted or attached decoration, such as the missing bronze bridles in I.31 – or the jewellery, which would almost certainly have been painted on, in I.61? There are no answers to such questions. But we need to remember, for instance, that, though most of the surviving sculptures are of marble, bronze (often inlaid and gilded) was more common: compare Plates I.37 and 82. And, finally, many famous works are known to us only from Roman copies (Plates I.26, 65, 69, 73, 83). Some thirty copies of the Doryphoros exist, but we can never be sure of the exact quality of the original!

If those technical problems are not enough, we still have to make the imaginative leap (and it does need imagination) between our perceptions and those of the Greeks. For instance, we still accept nude sculptures (male and female), though we do not accept nudity in public. In Greece, nude males were shown in sculpture and were acceptable in public, but females were always decently clothed (though often more revealingly shown in sculpture as the century progressed, and the first sculpted nude females date from the mid-fourth century).

We could argue that the very business of building temples and decorating them was a matter of reinforcing traditional values. Or we could claim that the abandonment of the formal poses of archaic work (compare Plates I.35, 37 with I.32, 34) represented a shift in values and greater concentration on the human. However, until we can be sure what the artists and patrons were aiming at, we are not in a good position to judge the results. We can however note the substantial change in the handling of figures during the fifth century. Compare Plates I.67 with I.70, and I.80 with I.83. We can also note that the sculptures of the Parthenon seem to mark a point of transition between a severe early style and what is known as the late classical style. Compare Plates I.31 and 32 with I. 35, and I.44–5 or I.84; also compare Plates I.33–4 with I.70, I.40, 68 and 71. Notice particularly the growing freedom of pose, the more fluid handling of drapery and the increasing realism of musculature.

But in a study of tension and change it is important to consider whether stylistic development is, or is not, significant change; and this is connected to the generally unanswerable question of whether a particular change can be related to other particular social or political changes. The burial of desecrated statues on the Acropolis following the Persian sack of Athens, for instance, is one of the useful dating points for sculpture; but it does not seem to mark any sudden stylistic development. Nor is there any clear change with the advent of Periclean democracy. Instead, figure sculpture seems to show a slow but steady development towards naturalism, first in the portrayal of individual parts of the body, then in the whole. But that is not to explain why Greek sculpture developed in this way, and I don't think we can get very far beyond the assertion that naturalism in Greek art is a reflection of the interest of the Greeks in the human condition and human nature. However, we can recognize that in mid-fifth-century Athens, a great deal of effort and considerable resources were devoted to the production of art. There was a lot of it about (as you can see from the Illustration Booklets!). And the next stage of our interpretation has to be a consideration of how the Greeks used art, who saw it and where. For that, we shall turn to two specific areas – grave *stelai* and votive monuments.

2.5 Private art: grave *stelai*

The Greeks commonly used carved gravestones, or *stelai*, to mark their graves. We could reasonably assume that these might tell us more about private art in contrast to the public sculptures of the Parthenon.

Look at the stelai *illustrated in Plates I.47–50 and I.56–63, and answer the following questions:*

1   *How do the* stelai *differ?*

2   *What can you infer from those differences?*

3   *By what sorts of criteria can we judge them?*

Discussion _____

Obviously my first two questions are linked so I will not separate discussion of them. All the *stelai* show figures carved in relief on a stone slab; and the most obvious change is from a tall narrow slab in the earlier examples (Plates I.47, I.59) to a broader, shorter one after about 430. This is a fairly major change of taste, and difficult to explain. Did you notice that in the later *stelai* there is a greater depth of relief, and space to portray a 'real' domestic scene? This sort of image would have been difficult on the narrow shape; but it would fit with a growing interest in naturalism and skill in representing it. If so, Plate I.48, with its archaic treatment of drapery, is an oddity! Yet that can be explained by its provenance. Thessaly was not the same as Attica; and, if Athens really was pre-eminent, you would expect better *stelai* there. But then how many of my examples are Attic? I have illustrated seven Attic examples and five from the rest of the Greek world. It is not merely a matter of selection. Following a relatively thin period, there seems to have been a flowering of *stelai* production in Athens after about 430.

After 430 it may well be that the war increased the market for *stelai*, but that does not fully explain the change in style. We evidently have to accept not only a market for more, but a taste for more elaborate tombstones after 430. It is, of course, the merest speculation, but could it be that more stonemasons and sculptors were free from engagements on the Acropolis after 430? (Check this against the dates and decoration of the Erechtheion and temple of Athene Nike!) Even if that was a factor in the change of style, we can, I think, also read a change in attitudes to the display of mourning, at least among those able to afford *stelai*.

A more interesting difference is the variety of scenes depicted. We might well expect private monuments to portray individually reminiscent moments. But how different are the faces shown? These images are so far from being portraits that we are often unsure which of the figures is the dead person. In fact portraiture was not common in fifth-century Athens.

Plates I.73 and 74 are two examples. But notice that the Pericles is a Roman copy and even the original was probably posthumous. It is likely that this head is thoroughly idealized. The head of Socrates is not securely dated and again, as you see from its present location, comes from the Roman world. It probably reflects later assessment of the famous snub-nosed philosopher. It is true that famous athletes and politicians were commemorated. Pausanias mentions a statue of Pericles on the Acropolis. But Pheidias caused a stir by carving a likeness of him on the shield of Athene Parthenos; and he so scandalized the Athenians by adding his own portrait that he was accused of sacrilege and left Athens to complete the cult statue of Zeus at Olympia.

I hope this makes clear that there are difficulties in drawing firm inferences from these *stelai*. We cannot even be sure of the status of the patrons, except that they must have been moderately wealthy. We are left therefore to judge the *stelai* aesthetically, as autonomous art works. Their quality clearly indicates the relative status of a particular patron or *polis*. There is a danger in acting on the assumption that they show scenes of *real* life. They certainly show *human* life as opposed to the life of gods and heroes, and presumably the scenes have some relevance to the departed. But notice how similar some of the compositions are (I.50, 61, 63). The addition of painted details might have made for more variety, but the similarity of composition and the general idealization of features suggests to me that these are generic rather than actual scenes designed for public consumption. And, of course, that would have been the case as the *stelai* were set up alongside the road out of Athens for all to see. In that case, criteria of size, richness and quality of carving (that is to say, largely aesthetic comparisons) may have been important to contemporaries, just as they are the only criteria for us. You might compare these *stelai* with the horsemen of the Parthenon frieze. ◆

2.6   Votive monuments

Sculpture is essentially a public art, and well suited to a society in which much of a man's life was lived in public. A votive sculpture is one dedicated to a god or goddess in fulfilment of a vow. Such works commemorated individuals and their feats, and often recorded the names of those who dedicated them.

Consider Plate I.64. How does it differ from the stelai *you have already studied?*

Discussion _____

In date it belongs with the earlier *stelai*, and uses a similar low relief technique. But how significant is the fact that it is not quite the same shape (nor is it as wide as the later *stelai*)? It is different from all the *stelai* you have studied in that it shows a goddess and was found on the Acropolis. Clearly this was not marking a private grave, but was some sort of public memorial. Pausanias records a great many such memorials, and they were obviously very much a part of Greek life. But as Lorna Hardwick suggests (Block 1, Section 6.1), it is even more difficult to interpret such scenes than to guess at personalities from the grave *stelai*. ◆

Now look at Plate I.72 which shows a votive relief from the sanctuary at Eleusis. How does this compare with (a) the stelai *you have studied and (b) the Parthenon frieze?*

Discussion _____

This large relief is a little later than the Parthenon frieze but earlier than the *stelai* in Plates I.61 and I.62. The subtle handling of drapery and flesh (particularly Triptolemos' shoulder and torso) mark this out as a work of quality. It seems to me at least as good, technically, as the Hegeso *stele* (Plate I.61) and rather better than Ampharete's (Plate I.62). On the other hand the relief is not quite as delicate or elaborate as the Parthenon frieze (having no overlapping forms, for example).

By its size this is an important dedication, and it comes from a major religious site (as you will see in TV7). If you accept my placing of the relief on the scale of quality, we may infer that public votive reliefs were generally finer than all but the best private grave *stelai*. That, of course, fits with the prestige that would be accorded to a public dedication such as the Eleusis relief, and the likelihood of a wealthy donor. The donor's name was recorded in an accompanying inscription. By contrast it is sometimes argued that the poor quality of a sculpture may be an indication that a particular work is a private funerary work rather than a public dedication. Of course it is dangerous to extrapolate from a single example; and public art has not always been the finest work available. Nevertheless it is generally accepted that in Classical Greece it was public art that represented the highest creative achievement. ◆

If items such as Plates I.64 and I.72 indicate the quality and status of votive sculpture, we need also to consider their quantity. Read the extract from Pausanias in the Supplementary Texts (ST 21c), and count the number of sculptures he refers to.

Discussion

I made it twenty named sculptures, which are all votive works except Zeus of the City and Artemis Brauronia, which are sanctuaries. But then Pausanias is describing the Acropolis, a sacred enclosure where one would expect a concentration of votive offerings. The excavation of the Agora, which you will see in TV6, showed Pausanias to be surprisingly accurate, and we know that he read the ancient sources, for he cites Thucydides. Since he is writing long after the completion of the Periclean Acropolis, he will be describing later offerings as well as contemporary; and unless he names the patron or sculptor we have little chance of sorting out the dates. He is also, understandably, selective. For instance, the small area of the steps of the West Court of the Parthenon indicates fittings for no fewer than thirty-eight votive *stelai* (see Plate I.90). Unfortunately we do not know what Pausanias' criteria for selection were.

Archaeology can also help. The Persian sack of Athens in 490 must virtually have cleared the Acropolis of votive monuments. Many, like Plate I.70, were found buried in a pit on the hill top, removed presumably because they had been sacrilegiously treated by the invaders. However, marble statues are more likely to survive than bronze (which can be melted down and re-used). Yet bronze dedications were probably more common, and we may get a false impression if we judge only from surviving marbles. At any rate, by the end of the fifth century there was evidently a large number of both reliefs and free-standing statues. Some of the sculptors' names are recorded, and we know roughly when they were working. Myron was at work around 450, and his son presumably some 20 years later. Alkamenes was also active in the last third of the century, while Kritios was working in the 470s. Kleiotas is also identified by Pausanias as a fifth-century sculptor. The fact that all the named sculptors in this extract are fifth-century clearly indicates the later Roman period's attitude to Classical Greece, and probably also suggests something about the quality of the works. ◆

The problem of copies also bedevils the study of Greek art. Plate I.84 was originally thought to be Greek of the Polykleitan period. It was found in Italy but could have been taken there by a Roman collector (the bronzes found in the sea, I.75–9, were presumably en route for Rome); but its similarity to lamp-holders from Pompeii now inclines scholars to believe it is Roman, though probably with some influence from fifth-century Greek work. (If that affects your view of its quality, consider the implications for your view of Greek art as a whole.) As it is we have to work from Roman copies as well as descriptions from the Roman period. Plates I.65 and I.69 are Roman copies, but they are generally accepted as copies of Myron's Athene and Marsyas mentioned by Pausanias.

One of the few Greek votive works that can be securely identified is the statue of Nike from Olympia, Plates I.71 and II.VI.

Look carefully at the image, and read extract ST 21d from Pausanias. Then answer these questions:

1   *Roughly where should this statue be placed in a chronological development of sculpture?*

2   *Does that dating help with the interpretation of Pausanias?*

3   *What can we learn from this statue about the importance of votive sculpture?*

Discussion

It is obviously more advanced in both pose and handling than the Euthydikos *kore* (Plate I.70). It is difficult to compare it with the Erechtheion Caryatid (Plate I.66) because its pose is not restricted by the double function as both statue and pillar (Plate I.18). Besides, this Nike is in motion and a better comparison might be the Nike relief (Plate I.40). The Paionios Nike seems to me a bit less delicate than that, but rather more free and dramatic than the flying Iris of the Parthenon (Plate I.34). It is generally dated soon after 421, that is a dozen or so years after the Parthenon, and before the Nike balustrade.

You might point out that we are comparing a work from Olympia with examples from Athens, and that we should take account of qualitative differences. Yet is it a work of quality? I must say, at once, that I personally rate this statue very highly indeed. Compare the handling of the drapery with the flying Iris (Plate I.34) and the Erechtheion Caryatid (Plate I.66). Comparing the drapery, I would also say it is rather better than Plate I.67 which is of much the same age, but from Athens. I think it also compares favourably with Plate I.87, from the Athenian Agora, which may have implications for our interpretation of this work, dedicated by the Messenians of Naupaktos! How and why did the Messenians come to commission a statue of this quality?

The Nike is, of course, a major dedication in one of the foremost sanctuaries of Greece. It was perched atop a triangular column some thirty feet high. Pausanias' doubts about the commemoration are interesting, though both actions, the siege of Oeniadai in 453 and the incident at Sphakteria in 425, belong to stages of the alliance between Athens and the Peloponnesian opponents of Sparta or Corinth. The first episode was under Pericles, and the second, described in great detail by Thucydides, effectively brought about the Peace of Nikias. The chronological date would agree with the claim Pausanias ascribes to the Messenians rather than the one he believes himself. But either story reinforces the Athenian link, and a public dedication of this sort, in a site within the Peloponnese, says a good deal about the prestige of the Athenian alliance *and* the openness of such international sanctuaries. ◆

Two more important statues, presumably part of a votive monument, have survived and are generally accepted as Phidian in style and possibly by the master himself. They cannot be securely identified with any known monument. They were recovered from a wreck off the Italian coast and were obviously on their way to some Roman imperial collection; but one theory is that they come from the sanctuary at Delphi.

Look carefully at Plates I. 77–79 and II.IV and II.V, and answer the following questions:

1   *How do these statues fit into the pattern of progress towards naturalism?*

2   *How do you rate them qualitatively?*

3   *What do they tell you about the nature of votive sculpture?*

Discussion

These bronzes are dated to the mid-century, and are just a little stiffer than, for instance, the Ilissos from the Parthenon (Plate I.32). They are stiffer than the Doryphoros or the Idolino boy (Plates I.83, 84), the originals of which were c.440–420. (But remember, the Idolino is no longer accepted as a copy and so should probably be discounted.) However, the warriors are clearly more confidently naturalistic than the Kritian boy (Plate I.80) – notice the hair and the musculature of the abdomen. The differences are fairly subtle, but they have most to do with the gradual loosening of the pose so that weight is realistically set on one leg, with the pelvis tilting towards the relaxed side, the spine curving and the shoulders tilting in the opposite direction. Compare this pose with that shown in *WA*, Figure 7:23. There was also in the fifth century a development towards an accepted canon of proportions (relation of head to height etc.). Polykleitos was a famous sculptor and rival of Pheidias who published a treatise on the subject (alas it does not survive), and his ideal man is shown in Plate I.83, a Roman copy of his famous spear-bearer. According to Pliny (*Natural History* 35.53), Polykleitos and Pheidias competed in designing an Amazon for the temple of Artemis at Ephesos, and Polykleitos won. Roman copies of their works survive (Plates I.85 and 86).

The Riace warriors compare well with the sculptures of the Parthenon. They are both superbly muscled, as you would expect of any warrior idealized on a monument. Their stance too is quite natural, and their faces more individual. Only their hair is rather formalized; but, if you think of it, a sculptor must formalize hair in some way in order to represent that particular material and texture in marble or bronze. The two warriors obviously held weapons and were part of a fairly elaborate composition of free-standing figures. There may well have been more than two, though we do not know what the composition was and we cannot be quite sure whether they were heroes or gods. Votive monuments were evidently quite elaborate affairs – something that is borne out by the surviving bases of the monuments, even when the sculptures are lost. And the technical achievement of casting figures seven feet high in bronze says a good deal about the effort that went into such monuments. Did you notice, too, that the eyes were inlaid with another material?

I have left my qualitative assessment till last, though you have to remember that it can colour your interpretation. These are very fine works. They were not designed to have the same delicacy and drama as the Nike; but I think the impression of strength and almost arrogant power is extraordinarily compelling. The sculptures are particularly important and exciting because they are the only extant bronze originals that may have been made by Pheidias. They can help us to gauge the quality of the Parthenon sculptures by comparison with other near contemporary dedications. However, it is likely that these bronzes are not Athenian: neither was the Nike of Paionios. ◆

Your final exercise in this section will involve some imagination since the monument no longer exists.

Read extract ST 21e from Pausanias, then look at Plates I.88–9, and answer the following questions:

1 *In the light of the sculptures you have already studied, what can you infer from this evidence about the quality and importance of this monument?*

2 *What does this monument and its function tell us about the function of sculpture in Athenian society?*

Discussion

The Monument of the Eponymous Heroes (name-heroes) was really the focus of civic emotion in Athens. It commemorated each of the ten tribes of Attica, and was set up in the Agora some time after 508. It was moved to the site shown in Plate 26 in the fourth century. There must presumably have been ten statues, perhaps rather like the Riace bronzes, and each must have been distinguished in some way (at the very least by an inscribed name). We do not know even the approximate date of the sculptures or the sculptor's name. Given the amount of redevelopment under Pericles, it would be easy to assume that they dated from the mid-fifth century. However, the fact that they were moved, rather than replaced, around 330 suggests that tradition and continuity, as opposed to novelty, were a part of the importance of this monument. Certainly the site and the size of the base make clear once again the centrality of votive sculpture in Athenian life.

But what I find most interesting is the association of heroic sculptures with the mundane but important function of the public notice-board. Notices relevant to each tribe were placed here, presumably under the appropriate figure, and almost daily commerce must have built for each Athenian citizen a strong sense of identification with an individual mythical figure. The sculpture was an integral part of his identity as a citizen. ◆

2.7 The place of art in Athenian society

You may feel that I have not got very far in interpreting the part played by the visual arts in Athenian culture. To what extent were the Athenians visually aware, and how far did art penetrate their society? These are questions to which there is no real answer. There was evidently a lot of 'art' about in votive monuments, temples and grave *stelai*. There were also wall paintings, a new development of the fifth century. None survives from Attica, but one of the most famous painters of antiquity was Polygnotos of Thasos, active 475–450, who became an Athenian citizen and was a friend of Kimon and possibly Sophocles. Pheidias, too, was a friend of Pericles, which goes to show the status of the leading artists. However, it does not tell us much about how 'art' was received. There are quite a few vivid descriptions in the literature, but the written evidence is not very helpful. What is clear is that they had rather different criteria of value from us. An important element was *mimesis* – literally, imitation. Art was seen as imitating an ideal, and providing examples for viewers to imitate. This could have a very profound effect on different media. Sculpture, being three-dimensional, might seem more real, a better mimesis, than two-dimensional painting. Yet painting seems to have grown in popularity and influence during the fifth century.

Look carefully at colour plates II.III–IV and you will notice a further important characteristic of Greek sculpture, the sense in which the heroes and gods had a sort of real presence. The eyes and lips are clearly coloured. In classical times the eyes, hair, lips and clothing of statues were regularly coloured. Some scholars believe that flesh was at least tinted as well (though natural marble can give a very flesh-like appearance). This is so different from our modern perceptions of sculpture, largely the result of conventions laid down in the nineteenth century, that we must constantly remind ourselves that we are not seeing the sculptures as the Greeks saw them.

Plato, in a well-known passage, sees art as having a very specific purpose. He seems to regard it as a vehicle for moral propaganda and nothing more. In the passage, Plato presents Socrates in discussion with an inquirer; the latter's responses are italicized.

Read the following extract and make brief notes on how Plato's view might relate to the sculptures we have studied.

> Thus, then, excellence of form and content in discourse and of musical expression and rhythm, and grace of form and movement, all depend on goodness of nature, by which I mean, not the foolish simplicity sometimes called by courtesy 'good nature', but a nature in which goodness of character has been well and truly established.
>
> *Yes, certainly.*
>
> So, if our young men are to do their proper work in life, they must follow after these qualities wherever they may be found. And they are to be found in every sort of workmanship, such as painting, weaving, embroidery, architecture, the making of furniture; and also in the human frame and in all the works of nature: in all these grace and seemliness may be present or absent. And the absence of grace, rhythm, harmony is nearly allied to baseness of thought and expression and baseness of character; whereas their presence goes with that moral excellence and self-mastery of which they are the embodiment.
>
> *That is perfectly true.*
>
> Then we must not only compel our poets, on pain of expulsion, to make their poetry the express image of noble character; we must also supervise craftsmen of every kind and forbid them to leave the stamp of baseness, licence, meanness, unseemliness, on painting and sculpture, or building, or any other work of their hands; and anyone who cannot obey shall not practise his art in our commonwealth. We would not have our Guardians grow up among the representations of moral deformity, as in some foul pasture where, day after day, feeding on every poisonous weed they would, little by little, gather insensibly a mass of corruption in their very souls. Rather we must seek out those craftsmen whose instinct guides them to whatsoever is lovely and gracious; so that our young men, dwelling in a wholesome climate, may drink in good from every quarter, whence, like a breeze bearing health from happy regions, some influence from noble works constantly falls upon eye and ear from childhood upward, and imperceptibly draws them into sympathy and harmony with the beauty of reason, whose impress they take.

(Plato, *Republic*, 3.400e–401d
tr. F.M. Cornford, *The Republic of Plato*, Oxford, 1942)

Discussion

Of course I have only presented a snippet of Plato's argument. We do not really know whether his view was absolute or whether he was reacting to what he saw as contemporary and unsatisfactory trends. For instance, could one see Plate I.37 as inspiring and I.71 as overblown and decadent? Equally we don't know whether Plato was particularly sensitive to the visual arts, though it could be significant that Socrates was trained as a stonemason. Finally there are no real grounds for assuming that Plato's views would have found widespread acceptance. Lorna Hardwick feels the reverse is more likely to be true; and it is important to remember that in the *Republic* Plato was writing a radical manifesto for an ideal *polis*. His is a fourth-century reaction to a fifth-century disaster, so his arguments there clearly cannot be taken at face value.

Nonetheless, Plato's notion of the close relationship between seeing works of art and moral development fits very closely with the sort of attitude we might assume to underlie the practice of setting up votive monuments. The city was literally peopled with representations of past heroes or commemorations of great events – perpetual reminders of the glories and duties of being an

Athenian. It might be part of the reason why so many of the faces appear to have been idealized (were all the Greeks handsome?), and why unflattering portraits were relatively scarce (the bust of Socrates illustrated in Plate I.74 may be an exception). ◆

This is a difficult and largely speculative area of discussion in which we shall not reach certainty. However, I think it is useful to remind ourselves that Greek art was 'other' than we are used to. Not only should it not be seen in pieces, in a museum context, but it was perceived in a rather different way.

3   VASE PAINTING

In this section, I want to look briefly at a completely different medium, vase painting – a more private art form with rather different functions, but important simply because so much survives. You will have noticed how many of the illustrations in *The World of Athens* are taken from vases. Ceramic is a material that is very difficult to destroy. Pots can be easily broken, but the pieces survive, whereas bronze can be easily melted down or marble burnt for lime. Very large numbers of Greek vases (or fragments) survive. Several hundred potters and painters are known by name (or identifiable as individuals), and a close analysis of the paintings allows a fairly secure dating of stylistic developments. Vases themselves can be used to provide a relative chronology for archaeologists. But, perhaps more important, the extraordinary richness of vase-painting as illustrative artwork is a phenomenon that was not repeated in the Western world until the majolica wave of the Renaissance.

Clearly there were, throughout the Greek world, many citizens of moderate wealth, for whom fine pottery was the height of luxury. Large amphorae filled with oil were awarded as prizes in the Panathenaic Games (these are so distinctive that they are regarded as a separate type, *WA* Figure 3:9 and Plates II.28–9). Since about the mid-sixth century, fine Attic pottery had been accepted as the best available, and exported to almost every Greek city, and to many places beyond the Greek-speaking world. By the fifth century, then, Athens had a well established trade and craft tradition. Many other *poleis* produced pottery, but Athens established the dominant style and had a virtual monopoly of quality. Compare Plates II.16 and II.18, and you will see how superior Attic painting was. This situation lasted at least until the end of the fifth century.

But just what was this craft, and what were the painted vases for? Such pots were certainly not the only ceramic products. There were roof tiles and architectural ornaments, terracotta statuettes (*WA* Figure 3:12) and coarse ware for wine jars and the like (Plates II.25–6 and *WA* Figure 5:9). Though very large quantities of fine pottery survive, it was clearly a luxury trade and reserved for rather special occasions. We can get some idea of this by considering the common shapes and their functions.

However, we need to assess the place of painted pottery in fifth-century Athenian life, and to consider how we can use it as evidence and what for.

INTERACTIVE

First turn to Cassette 3, Band 4, 'Material evidence II: Vase painting', for some basic information about pots. As always, refer closely to examples in the Illustration Booklets.

3.1 The progress of painting style

Your study of the cassette material should have shown you some of the skills used by specialists in analysing Greek vase painting. I want you now to look at the broad sweep of change in painting style over the century, and to study nine vases chosen from different dates – Plates II.33, 34, 36, 35, 37, 38, 39, 40 and 19.

I have tried to select typical rather than especially fine examples. What changes in style can you detect over the century? Are there any other changes? You will need to compare details carefully.

Discussion ────────────────────────────

The easiest change to spot is probably the drapery. At first it is painted in straight pleats, then in more natural curves and finally swirling about and freely drawn. At first, too, the muscles are drawn with hard firm lines; but by the end of the century the drawing is freer. Small details change too. At first eyes are drawn full-frontal in profile faces. Profile eyes begin to appear by about 470. After 470 three-quarter views became more common, especially of a hand or a foot; and there is a great variety of poses. After 450 the profile view was more popular but three-quarter views were more confidently handled. There are other changes too. For instance, in the later vases figures do not all stand on the same plane or on the same level, and there are indications of landscape (more realism). In the earlier vases, too, the composition is more closely geared to the shape of the pot with the figures arranged to make an attractive pattern. ◆

Obviously this exercise will not equip you to undertake stylistic analysis on your own; and our sample is impossibly small anyway. However, I hope you can see what is involved.

We can now begin to ask questions about these changes, their relationship to other art forms and other developments during the century.

First of all, compare Plates I. 70 with II.31, I.33 with II.30, I.87 with II.41. Can you trace a parallel development in sculpture and vase painting?

Discussion ────────────────────────────

In some ways the developments are closely parallel. The two earlier pieces show similar delight in rather stiff patterning, particularly in the folds of drapery. Similar heavy folds are shown in the two mid-century examples; but here a difference creeps in. The Parthenon sculptors use the folds across the form to reveal the solid body beneath. The vase painter, working in two dimensions, still uses his folds to create a pattern, though this time a freely flowing one. By the end of the century sculptural drapery is deeply cut and freely, even wildly, flowing, giving a heightened sense of drama. My late fifth-century vase is much simpler, and the drawing almost perfunctory. You can see a similar trend if you compare Plates I.80 and II.49 with I.44 and II.59. ◆

Obviously it is not safe to make bold comparisons between works of such different status as a humble *lekythos* (II.41) and a public dedication (I.87). However, my examples do reflect one aspect of the stylistic history of Greek art. The quality of votive sculpture seems to have remained high, at least until the end of our period. On the other hand, it is generally agreed that vase painting declined in quality as the century progressed, that the peak of the red figure style was around 470 and that after 440 it was declining into a minor art. In fact by the end of the century local manufacturers were beginning to eat into the Attic export market (II.20). The parallel rise of wall painting, which we know from literary sources, is cited as part of the reason; and vases such as Plate II.2 are seen as evidence of the influence of illusionist painting with the use of perspective (notice the figure collapsing behind the rock, bottom right). There is some strength in the argument that the drawing on the later vases is not as careful as on the earlier ones. And I would argue that the compositions which take less account of the shape of the pot are less satisfactory. But you might argue that the organization of scenes in bands, as in II.9, is an improvement on II.12 or II.49. This is partly a matter of personal taste, I suppose. But remember also that the single viewpoint of the camera does not favour single figures drawn round the curve of a pot. They were designed to be enjoyed by the moving eye, on pots that could themselves be moved. It is probably better to regard the Meidias hydria (II.9) as part of a growing taste for elaboration in which, again, vase painting may have been influenced by the scope and palette of wall painting. However, I think the general decline in vase painting is clear enough if you compare the late examples of II.16, II.19, II.39 and II.48 with early examples such as II.6, II. 33 or II.45.

Of course, my examples are not entirely parallel. It would be fairer to compare II.15 and II.19, which are both *aryballoi*. But what effect does acceptance of the trend have on our understanding of the pots? It should come as a bit of a jolt to find a decline in a major art form during the years of Pericles' ascendancy, though perhaps decline after 430 is less surprising. But you should be careful not to assume too great an importance for the pottery industry. Some two-fifths of all Attic vases from the fifth century have been securely ascribed to about 500 painters and workshops and that total is not likely to increase much. Assuming a working life of about 25 years for a painter, this implies that no more than about 100–125 vase-painters were at work at any one time. Hardly a major force!

3.2   The function of Greek vases

At this point we need to ask what this workforce was making and painting, and how their productions fitted into Attic or Greek society. Vases are easily categorized by shape and we know what most of the shapes were for.

Look at Plates II.2, 3, 4, 6, 8, 9, 11, 12, 19, 22 and 36, as well as Plate 10 in the TV and Audio-cassette Illustrations, a selection of the most typical shapes. What can you infer from these about the ways and circumstances in which Greek painted pottery was used?

Discussion

The *amphora, pelike* and *stamnos* are all large jars; but the fact that they are decorated means that they were for use at feasts and parties rather than just for storage. Compare them with Plates I.28 and II.25 and 26. Plate II.25 and 26 are plain storage jars, while the Panathenaic prize *amphorae* were given full of oil. Both of these types have a narrower neck that could be easily sealed up. The *hydria* was a water jar with a third handle for pouring (concealed behind the neck in Plate II.9), and the *krateres* were used for holding water and mixing it with wine. But, again, notice the size. A *krater* twenty-one inches high would hold gallons rather than pints of liquid (I know of no reliable study of the cubic contents of these jars). The *oinochoe*, whose very name means wine-pourer, and the cups are also designed for drinking parties. And the cups are substantially larger than the average wine glass today, though just as elegant. The *kylix*, in particular, is a technically daring piece of the potter's craft. Evidently these vases were for use at parties where a good deal of liquid was drunk. Only the white ground *lekythoi* and the *aryballoi* were for other purposes. The *lekythoi* were dedicated at tombs (in Plate II.50 you can see one resting on the painted tomb), and the *aryballoi*, which are quite the smallest items, were for scented oil with which an athlete might anoint himself, once again a luxury use.

Other shapes such as the small flask, or *askos*, in the shape of a lobster's claw, II.42, were probably also for perfume and clearly designed for show and pleasure rather than function. All these shapes were designed specifically for luxury use, for special occasions. They are also, incidentally, largely for the use of male citizens. The *pyxis*, II.24 and II.XII, was a toilet box for women; but we shall return to the different depictions of women on these, and vases such as II.48, later.

The quality of such items tells us a good deal about the nature of Greek society; though we must assume that, being luxury wares, they were cherished, and had a better survival rate than their humbler counterparts. The fact that they were designed for a particular sector of society should also warn us of the decided slant we may get by using them, and the pictures on them, for evidence about society as a whole. Yet the very fact of their survival means that they are an important element of the archaeological evidence, as well as fascinating, and often beautiful, items in their own right. ◆

I'd like you now to look at the captions in Illustration Booklet II and consider the provenance of the vases. Does that tell us any more about the function of Attic vase painting?

Discussion

The enormous majority were found outside Attica. In my sample, only the vases illustrated in II.15, 16, 23, 39, 43, 51–3 and II.XII–XVI are from sites within the *polis* compared with over thirty from Sicily and South Italy. There is a contrast of quality too. II.53 shows a very simple early fifth-century vase such as were buried in ordinary citizens' graves. (You can see a similar one lying by the body in Figure 10.) This one is not of comparable quality with II.51; but even so it seems that the best-quality vases are from overseas, many from Etruscan tombs. Fine-quality ware was certainly used in Attica, for instance II.39 and II.XII, or II.43. However, it seems to me significant that some of the finest vases from Attica are the funerary *lekythoi* (II.23 and II.XIV and II.51). These white ground *lekythoi* only became common in the second half of the fifth century, and the type disappeared after *c*.400. But the quality of the drawing is often very high. Perhaps we should relate these to the development of funerary monuments that began in the last third of the century. ◆

Figure 10 Attica. Skeleton and funerary vases from cemetery at Laureion. First half of the fifth century.

Further excavation may change the picture a little, but the main point is clear – Attic red figure pottery was a luxury item with a strong export market. If you accept that the best work was produced between *c*.475 and *c*.450, it would also be tempting to link that with the growth of Athenian influence after the Persian Wars. There is undoubtedly some truth in this, but only some. Attic pottery had been established as the best in Greece since the mid-sixth century; so the extent of the export market in the fifth century was not new. The decline in quality towards the end of the century was.

3.3   Interpretation

We are left with the final problem of interpreting the scenes on vases. No other society has used such a wide range of scenes, from myths of gods and heroes (II.1) to the intimate details of everyday life (II.40), or used them so consistently as the Greeks. And the sheer survival of vases makes them attractive as evidence for all sorts of aspects of Athenian life. In this final section, I can offer no certainty, but only suggest possibilities and warn of some of the dangers. There is, first, the problem of the applicability of evidence. Of the eighty-four illustrations from vase painting in *The World of Athens*, only nineteen are of pots from 470–400, whereas forty-one are from vases dated 500–470. I would suggest that this leaves us with two insoluble problems of which we need to beware. First, we should be cautious of the date of any piece of evidence before we place too much reliance on it. Second, we need to take account of the changes of taste in decoration. Quite a large proportion of the well-known scenes of everyday life are from black figure vases (e.g. *WA* I.3, I.5, I.7, I.11 and Illustration Booklet II.58). Can we be sure they are applicable to the fifth century? The existence of later examples of everyday scenes such as II. 59–61 suggests that we can, but we must obviously be cautious.

Finally there is the question of the interpretation of the scenes.

Turn to Plate II.43. What are the problems of using items such as this for evidence of women's roles?

Discussion

Since Iphigenia and Danae do not occur in the same myth, we can accept that this is not a mythical scene. It shows women at home – the door is presumably that of the women's quarters. I am not quite sure what the things are hanging behind the door (there is often the problem of recognition). But one of the women appears to be doing something to her hair, while the other is carrying a box of jewellery. Since this is a toilet box, it is a woman's object. But, do the scenes represent what women were commonly restricted to? Or, since the *pyxis* was presumably bought by the husband, do they show what men thought the women ought to be restricted to? There is no answer to that, though a wider survey does show other images of women in a similar role – for example, I.61 or II.13 and II. 41. (But in II.41 she is bringing the basket to a young man.) Women are also shown at drinking parties, as in II.48; recent scholarship usually claims that such scenes depicted non-citizen women, engaged in entertainment and/or prostitution. Both roles, however, reinforce our view of the chauvinism that underlay Attic society. You might look for evidence elsewhere to support this view. ◆

Changes in the choice and content of scenes may also be significant. However, it is much more difficult to link these to the movement of ideas or changes in the political situation. Certainly scenes of Greeks fighting Persians occur soon after Marathon; but in changes to mythological scenes we might expect to find more subtle comments. Professor J. Boardman (*Attic Red Figure Vases: the Archaic Period*, Thames and Hudson, 1985) has pointed out how in the first half of the century Herakles (II.3, 12), the hero of Peisistratan Athens, is replaced by Theseus (II.8, 37), the hero of Athenian democracy. Dionysos and his maenads are predictably popular in drinking vessels. But what are we to make of the many Nikai? Are they reflections of specific victories, or merely a generalized triumphalism? And there are problems of identification too. Does II.11 represent Nike (who has wings) or Artemis (who is usually shown with a deer or as a huntress)?

Figure 11a

Figure 11b

Figure 11c a–c Attic red figure kylix from Vulci Etruria 9, (a) interior: Hephaistos and Thetis; (b) and (c) exterior: foundry workers, by the Foundry painter, *c.*480–475 (diameter 30.5cm., 12in.) (Cat.2294; ARV 400.1). This sort of vase is typical of those that are attractive as sources for 'everyday life' in Athens. The scenes in the foundry are full of interesting details. Notice the boy behind the furnace working the bellows; and the designs hanging on the wall above him. But it is unwise to use these images as direct description. Consider how important pattern is in the composition in plate (c), and how that relates to the scale of the figures. Presumably the image is of two clients, two workers and a statue; and scale may be used to indicate importance. Or compare figure (a) with plate II.60. How does one distinguish the god Hephaistos from a mortal helmet-maker? Hephaistos was the god of craftsmen, but without inscriptions we can only suggest what is likely. In this case there is an inscription but it is a dedication to a lover (the word KALOS can be made out). Yet the scene, with a woman receiving the weapons, does not look as realistic as the exterior scenes, so the equation with the story from the Trojan War seems perfectly reasonable.

I find it significant that more violent scenes from the Trojan War (*WA* 3:1–8, 2:2 and 2:11) are replaced with less active images or episodes in the mid-century (II.21, II.24). I believe this is an indication of a different attitude to warfare. After Marathon, victory made the agony of struggle and the tragic part of the Homeric cycle exciting. In the mid-century the isolation of the Achilles figure suggests a more thoughtful attitude, recognizing the nobility of the hero as an individual. The Judgement of Paris could reflect an interest in the causes of conflict, as well as being more appropriate to women's use. However, I hope it is clear that this is highly speculative, and that the evidence of vase painting is not enough on its own. It *is* evidence but its value is in the way it corroborates or conflicts with other evidence, from archaeology, philosophy, history or drama.

At this point I suggest you pause, look back at the three guiding questions set out in the study guide to Sections 2 and 3 (pp.12–13) and write a few paragraphs summarizing your response. You might find it particularly useful to think about the *differences* in the pace and direction of change in public and private art. Are changes happening at different times in (say) public architecture and in vase painting? Did you find evidence of fundamental changes in the role and function of art and architecture in society as a whole, or are we dealing with technical and stylistic developments rather than radical change? Do differences in the amount, prominence, subject-matter and presentation of art and architecture at different points in the century amount to *changes*? Are the

causes of these variations important? These would be useful questions to discuss in a tutorial or self-help group.

Now turn to the Offprints and read the article by F. Lissarrague, *'Epiktetos egraphsen*: the writing on the cup'.

Further Reading

CARPENTER, T.H. (1991) *Art and Myth in Ancient Greece*, Thames & Hudson.

ROBERTSON, M. (1992) *The Art of Vase Painting in Classical Athens*, Cambridge University Press.

SPARKES, B.A. (1996) *The Red and the Black: studies in Greek pottery*, Routledge.

SPIVEY, N. (1996) *Understanding Greek Sculpture: ancient meanings, modern readings*, Thames & Hudson.

SPIVEY, N. and RASSMUSSEN, T. (eds) (1991) *Looking at Greek Vases*, Thames & Hudson.

4 PHYSICAL ENVIRONMENT AND SOCIO-ECONOMIC FACTORS

Study guide

Before studying this section it is essential to have worked through Cassette 2, Bands 1–3; Cassette 3, Bands 1–3; and the accompanying notes. While working on the section you will need to use *WA*, *ST* and Illustration Booklet II. We shall indicate where it is necessary for you to refer to a source. Other references are for information and to help you in revising.

The aim of this section is to approach some of the important aspects of the physical and socio-economic environment of the Athenians.

In Sections 2 and 3, you did detailed work on specialized areas of the material environment of the Athenians – art, artefacts and architecture. In this section, I am going to broaden out the concept of the environment to include physical aspects, the use made of natural and human resources, and the impact of events – whether natural or human. We will be looking at the material framework within which the Athenians lived and at some of the stresses to which it was subject during the fifth century.

Five topics have been selected with the intention of helping you to develop your own judgements about the relationships between stability, tension and change which form the overall theme of the block. These topics are:

1   Land use

2   Slavery

3   Wealth

4   The benefits of empire

5   The effects of war on the Athenians

We have used specific questions to help your study of the separate topics. These provide guidance which will help you to analyse and compare the evidence offered by different sources. If you wish you can work on each topic separately. However, at some point you will need to stand back from the material and relate it to the overall theme of the whole block – tensions and change in the fifth century. You may decide to do this after studying each topic (I have included a reminder) or at the end of the block. The important thing is to have a definite plan. The Revision Block, Block 6, will include exercises helping you to develop your own judgements based on the evidence you have studied.

To help you relate your detailed work on each topic to the overall themes of the block, we suggest you continue to use the three guiding questions:

1   What is the contribution of this topic in a study of the material environment?

2   Can we use evidence gleaned from this topic to approach other aspects of Athenian life and attitudes?

3   How does evidence from this topic help us to study change in the fifth century? What kind of change/changes are we meeting? Or does the evidence point to stability?

Each topic is designed to be manageable in a study session of about one and a half hours. However, you will probably find that Topic 1 takes more time and Topics 4 and 5 slightly less time.

4.1   Topic 1: Land use

4.1.1 Soil, topography and food supply

Please read WA 1.11–13 and 1.20–21 and look at Illustration Booklet 2, Plates VII–XI.

Plates II.X and XI show something of the range of Greek agriculture. The steep hillside in II.XI is as difficult to cultivate as any in the upper Rhine, and the vines are small. Yet in 1961 it was producing fine grapes. I.X, the plain of Argos, is flat and laid out in a dense pattern of fields. Today it is one of the most fertile parts of Greece, yet even there in summer all is brown and the rivers dry up before they reach the sea. Attica, as Menander suggests (*WA* p.70), was less fertile. Plate II.VII shows how green the cereal-growing part of Attica can get in the brief spring, but notice how stony the ground is and how suddenly fields give way to rocky hillside. II.VIII shows an area that is among the best farmland in Attica. Even so the aridity is noticeable. Compare these young olives with the mature trees shown in *WA* Figure 1:8. Today this area grows excellent fruit, grapes, vegetables and nuts; but how can we extrapolate to the fifth century BCE? (Cassette 2, Band 3 suggests some possibilities.) Plate II.IX seems to match exactly Plato's comment (*WA* p.75); yet there are reasons for believing it was much more heavily wooded in the fifth century. The early furnace sites at Laureion adjoin the mine shafts and so were presumably kept supplied with local firewood. By the fourth century large furnace complexes (one is 180 metres long!) were built on the coast. Presumably by then they had to be supplied with imported timber and it was more economical to cart the ore to the coast for smelting. In that case Plato's image of a land wasted by disease might be a description of a change he actually witnessed.

To Western European eyes, the account in *WA* and the illustrations may seem to support each other. We tend to associate fertility with high rainfall and lushness. But successful peasant subsistence agriculture is characterized by other features – selection of crops adapted to local fluctuations in soil and climate, diversification in crops, dispersed location of holdings and the use of appropriate sites and methods for storage. Recent research suggests that the ability of Attica to make at least a significant contribution to her grain needs may have been underestimated. In addition, the remains of ancient terracing may suggest that cultivation in antiquity was more extensive than nowadays.

Nevertheless, it is true that when Athens in the fifth century became the centre of a prosperous empire, both the volume and pattern of demand changed. Agriculture was called on to do more than provide subsistence for the existing population. The population grew, especially in the urban centres, partly as the result of attracting trade and workers from other states. It is a paradox that while imperialism provided a means of averting food supply crisis (by controlling sea routes and facilitating the grain trade), it also increased the risks of crisis by concentrating population and lengthening supply lines.

Look at Course Guide Maps 2 and 3 for an indication of the main grain-importing routes.

The lack of food riots in democratic Athens, the relative absence of coercive laws to control the grain trade (although other forms of intervention were used – for example, Old Oligarch 2.2–3, *ST* 28), the fact that the tithes of empire were collected in cash, not grain, and the fact that from the 420s partial abandonment of the Attic countryside was a viable proposition, suggest that the arrangements for the regular importation of grain worked satisfactorily. However, a supply which relies on the efficiency of distribution mechanisms is always vulnerable to natural hazards (such as harvest shortfall or epidemic disease) or to human interventions, such as prolonged war. This point is recognized by Thucydides when he portrays Nikias opposing the Sicilian expedition because the Syracusans had an advantage in possessing home-grown corn (Bk.6, 20, 4). At the end of the Peloponnesian War the lack of an adequate home supply meant that blockade resulted in starvation and defeat for Athens. (See *WA* H.I.56 in conjunction with *WA* Map 4 for the key significance of the Athenian defeat at Aigospotamoi in 405.)

4.1.2 Land-holding and the law

Law can yield important evidence since it provides a formal expression of public beliefs about desirable and undesirable conduct. The Athenian system was the first to be established on a democratic base and we may therefore take it as a practical expression of the application of democracy to important areas of public life. Unfortunately only a small number of texts of actual laws survive. Evidence is otherwise derived indirectly, from law court speeches (mainly dating from *c.*435–322 but with the emphasis on the fourth century) and from allusions in other texts, especially comedy and history.

There are two important points about land-holding in the fifth-century Athenian *polis*. The first is that ownership and inheritance of land were restricted to citizens. Exceptions were rare and had to be specially approved. Inheritance was from father to son or to the nearest male heir. Legitimacy and citizenship were therefore vital in establishing rights to property, and evidence from forensic speeches shows that disputes were energetically pursued (for a fourth-century example, see *WA* 4.18–20).

The second point is that there was remarkable freedom from collective political unrest about land. Peasant proprietors and wealthy landowners appear to have reconciled their interests, although archaeologists disagree about the balance between smallholdings and larger estates. Even the chaos at the end of the fifth century does not appear to have been fuelled by disputes about the distribution of land. The Aristotelian *Constitution of Athens* comments on this contrast with other *poleis* (see *ST* 6, 40.3).

One specialized aspect of land-holding was of particular importance to the Athenians. This concerns exploitation of the mines. The exact legal status of the mines is a matter of dispute. However, the evidence suggests that the *underground* area was considered to be the property of the state, and that those wishing to open up or work a mine negotiated it with the *poletai* (officials responsible for sales of state property). Fragmentary inscriptions of the accounts of the *poletai* record leases, naming the mine, location, purchaser and price (see Figure 12). There are also references in written texts to the purchase of leases (for example, ?Aristotle, *Constitution of Athens* 47).

The legal position of the land surface above the mine is less clear. The *poletai* accounts sometimes identify a mine as in 'X's estate', but we do not know if the landowner received payment for disturbance to agriculture or whether he was likely to become the lessee. The workshops situated near the mines were owned by individuals, and a law made it an offence to 'exclude from the operations', i.e. to withhold access. TV4 is a case study of the archaeological evidence about mining activity at Laureion.

Figure 12 Inscription from the Athenian Agora recording a mine lease.

4.1.3 Changes in land use in the fifth century

There are a number of controversial issues here. I have already mentioned the dispute about the point at which Athens became crucially dependent on imported grain. However, *that* problem implies a change in the pattern of demand rather than a change in agricultural production. The question of land use applies just as much to the way *urban* sites were developed and used. *WA* 1.21 drew our attention to the importance of local centres and loyalties in rural Attica but suggested that there was increased urbanization during the century.

The concept of urbanization is in itself a complex one, but for our purposes here we can distinguish three aspects:

1 An increasing emphasis on the city itself as the centre for political activity (we shall be focusing on this in Part 2 of this block, Section 6).

2 A degree of enforced urbanization of the population because of the war and especially because of Pericles' policy of partial evacuation of Attica. (This will be considered in Topic 5 below.)

3 Positive growth in urban activity in response to economic pressures. The prime example of this is the development of the Piraeus (harbour, walls, dockyards, commercial buildings, housing, attraction of *metics*: see *WA* 1.23). The written sources tend to emphasize the role of Piraeus as an urban base not just for imperial activities but also for the developed democracy, sometimes emphasizing its separateness from Athens – for example, when referring to 403, both Xenophon and Lysias use the phrase 'the men of Piraeus' to describe those who continued to defend democracy, as a contrast to the phrase 'the men of the asty [town]' which denotes those who were governed by the Thirty Tyrants. However, this association with democratic resistance perhaps obscures the real issue, which is the nature and purpose of the

development of the Piraeus earlier in the fifth century. Archaeological evidence is an important counterweight to the political emphasis of the written sources since it enables us to study the chronology, function and quality of development.

Now look back to the study guide at the beginning of this section and see if you want to add any comments in response to the three guiding questions I suggested.

In the next sub-section Colin Cunningham will ask you to look closely at some of the archaeological evidence on rural settlement and urban development. This will draw on the plan-reading skills you developed when working on Cassette 3, Band 2, so please refer back to this now if you need to refresh your memory.

4.1.4 Urban development: Piraeus

The men of the city and the men of Piraeus may have been regarded as distinct entities politically. Was there a basis for this difference in their physical environment? And how did that develop during the fifth century? Piraeus ought to be a tempting study since it was a creation of the fifth century.

Read the description in WA 1.23–4 and look at Figures 1:10 and 6:14. What strike you as the 'modern' features of Piraeus, and how do they differ from Athens?

Discussion

The fact that it was a naval town obviously distinguished it from the city; and *WA* points out that there would have been different inhabitants. That it was new and laid out on a grid plan was also distinctive, though I suppose parts of it must have echoed the Acropolis in that they were building sites for much of the century. It would be tempting to draw a parallel between Edinburgh (ancient, prosperous and respectable) and the town of Leith (overcrowded and, in repute at least, far from respectable). However, we should remember that this seaport was the home of the Athenian navy, mainstay of Athenian imperial power. To some extent, therefore, it will have been a favoured place; but its fortunes will have varied as the navy waned. During the years when the ships were in Samos, Piraeus may have become something of a ghost town; and that might account for the political dichotomy.

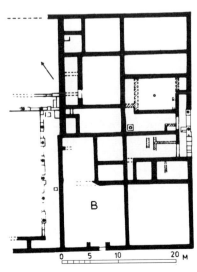

Figure 13 Piraeus. Plan of block of houses under modern theatre

Figure 14 Olynthos, Chalkidike. Plan of blocks of houses c.430–380 BCE.

47

Another important factor is that, as a port, Piraeus must have been in close contact with, and to some extent judged by, other cities of the ancient world. Perhaps this was one of the reasons why Pericles brought Hippodamos of Miletos to plan the town. The new city of Miletos (which became one of Athens' allies) was laid out by Hippodamos in about 470 with a regular grid of straight streets (four or eight metres wide), and a centrally placed agora. The relative importance of Athens and Miletos might well have made Pericles keen to have a port at least as well planned. The Hippodamian principle of town-planning spread to the whole Greek world, and became the accepted standard by about the end of the fifth century.

In Piraeus, archaeological evidence has revealed a regular street pattern, though the grid was adjusted to accommodate the steeper slopes of Akte. There was an agora by the main harbour, where the two principal streets crossed at right angles. In addition the public buildings included the ship-sheds by each harbour. On the slopes of Akte one street has been traced with cross streets making regular blocks of about 60 metres frontage with, apparently, two houses to each block. One block of houses further north was partly excavated many years ago, and gives some idea of the layout (Figure 13). The rectangular block is divided into four by cross walls making four dwellings. The two on the right have a shared entrance porch. To the left is part of a large pillared court, perhaps a semi-public garden. But the excavation did not record all the partition walls and doorways (look for the entrance to the top left-hand house), or the stages of rebuilding, so these houses are difficult to date and we cannot be sure of the precise plan. What is clear is that they were part of a regularly planned grid of blocks. However, the best evidence for this sort of development comes, not from Attica, but from a suburb of Olynthos (Figure 14), where houses were laid out in blocks of about 100 × 40 metres. Each house plot was about twenty metres square and they were arranged back-to-back in rows with a narrow alley between. This plan was probably similar to the plan at Piraeus; but we assume that it was more sophisticated, in that Olynthos was laid out in 430 BCE and not fully built until the early fourth century. ◆

4.1.5 Urban development

Now look at Figure 15. How is this different from Piraeus?

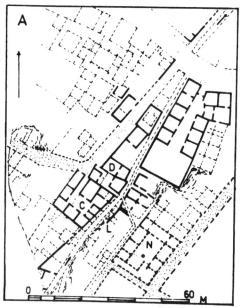

Figure 15 Athens, the industrial district. Plan showing houses D, C, L and N and work-shops, fifth century. House N. Roman period.

Discussion _____

This housing is from Athens, and the irregular street pattern is apparent. Even in the ancient world Athens was recognized as old and irregular. And Demosthenes made the point that in contrast to the public buildings, the individual houses were not grand:

In public life they [the worthies of old] created for us edifices and ornaments of such quality and scale in the form of temples and dedications within them, that none of their successors have been able to surpass. But in private life they were so temperate and so true to the spirit of the constitution that if anyone here present knows which is the house of ARISTIDES or that of MILTIADES or of any outstanding man of that time, he will see that these are in no way more grand than those of their neighbours.

(Demosthenes, *Olynthiac*, 3.iii.25–6)

Of course since our example is from a site on the slopes of the Areopagus, it may be more than usually irregular. However, it is from such areas that most of our knowledge of Athenian housing in fact comes. Some 100 house sites within the walls of ancient Athens are known, which must only be a small proportion of the whole. Yet of that hundred only a tiny fraction has been fully excavated, so our evidence is scanty. Nonetheless we can assume from Thucydides' description of the overcrowding at the start of the Peloponnesian War (Thucydides Book 2) that the city was pretty fully built up. So what does our evidence suggest? ◆

Look at Figures 16, 17, 18, 19 and 20. What can you deduce from these about housing in fifth-century Athens?

Discussion

First, I hope you noticed the variety and irregularity of the plans. You can see a trend towards regularity if you compare House (a) in Figure 18, which was rebuilt about 480, with House (c), which is of the mid-fifth century. In fact this one conforms most nearly to Piraeus or Olynthos houses. However, the trend to regularity was constrained by the irregular layout of streets and alleys. My latest example, Figure 20, has a thoroughly irregular exterior, though the interior is more ordered. ◆

You probably also noticed how the houses were laid out round an internal courtyard, sometimes with a well (Figure 17C and Figure 18a), sometimes with a portico or verandah (Figure 17D), though regular colonnades seem to be later. The actual use of the rooms is more difficult to decide. Several of the houses had bathrooms, and notice the room in Figure 18b at the south-east corner of the courtyard. This shows the raised platform for the dining couches, and was clearly the *andron* or men's dining room (its use is shown in Plate II.45). We can be sure that each house had one, and in the houses in Figure 18a and c they may well have been in similar positions at the south-east of the court. In each case this room is square and one of the largest rooms in the house. The plan of Figure 19 is altogether different; but did you notice the steps to the left? This house is on a steep slope, which governs the design. In fact the rear rooms are semi-basement. Notice the curving entrance stairs.

You may also have noticed that I have talked exclusively of plans, although you have reconstructed views. Remains such as those in Figure 16 give us the plan; and these houses usually have stone wall bases. Above that the walls were of mud brick with tiled roofs, of which only fragments remain. We cannot even be sure if there were upper storeys, but have to guess from the thickness of the walls. Excavations can also tell us a bit about the way of life in these houses. Those in Figure 17 are in what is called the Street of the Marble Workers or the Industrial Quarter from the remains of marble and bronze working found in them. They were both home and workshop. Figure 16 is clearly a very modest house, but it was also home and workshop – evidence of cobblers' work was found. The house stands near the Agora – you can see the *horos* or boundary stone against the north wall in the centre foreground – and it has been confidently identified as the house of Simon the Shoemaker, friend of Socrates. Among the finds from it was the base of a cup inscribed 'Simon's'. ◆

Figure 16 Athens, near Agora. Excavated remains of the house of Simon the Shoemaker with reconstruction. Fifth century.

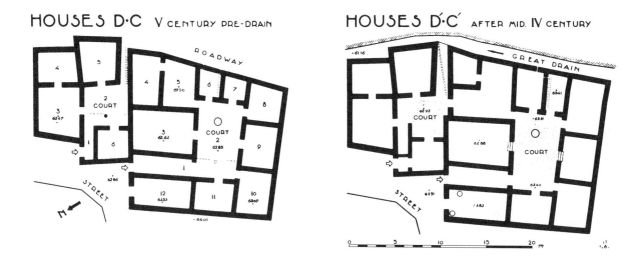

Figure 17 Athens, near Agora. Houses D and C, plan, fifth century.

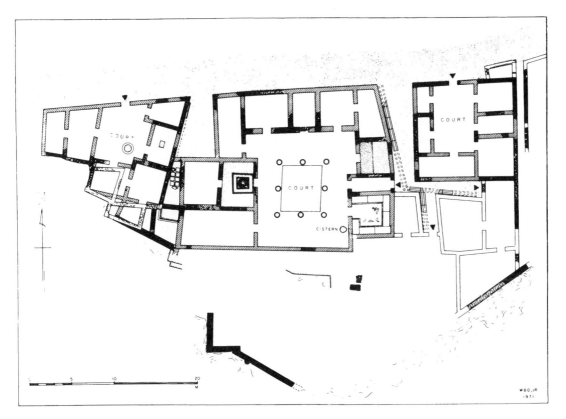

Figure 18 Athens, west of the Areopagus. Plan of three houses. Fifth–fourth century, (a) left: *c*.490 destroyed 480 and rebuilt, altered late fifth century, (b) centre: *c*.325, (c) right: *c*.460–450.

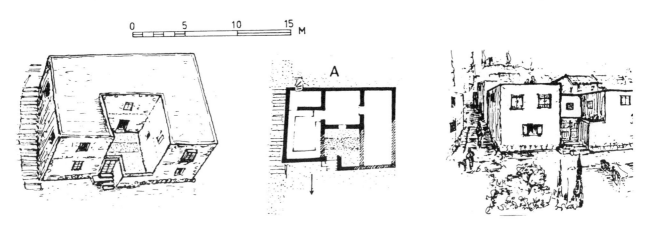

Figure 19 Athens north-east slope of Pynx. Plan and reconstructed views of house, probably fifth century.

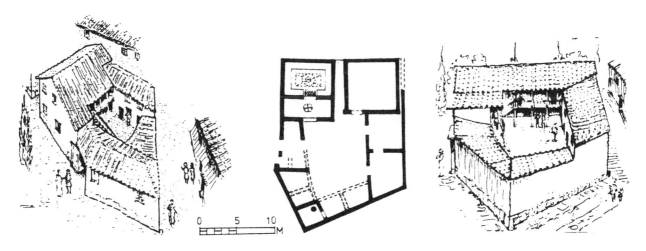

Figure 20 Athens, west of Areopagus. House of the Greek mosaics, *c*.300. Reconstructed ground plan and perspective views.

4.1.6 Housing outside Athens

Provincial urban housing

The picture of irregularity, simplicity and gradual rebuilding in the city is clear enough even from our small sample. Fortunately we also have in Attica another urban site at Thorikos, a town that grew up in the fifth century and declined after the fourth. The remains there are the largest area of housing so far excavated in Attica. *Look at Plate I.93 and Figures 21 and 22. What can you learn from these about Attic housing?*

Discussion

The first thing to remember is that Thorikos was a provincial mining town. You can see at once that it does not have any of the regularity of Piraeus. In Figure 21 you can see the industrial element, the washing table, in the midst of the housing, though it is in a separate building. But this is really no different from the situation in Figures 16 or 17. The house is laid out round a court with the *andron* a large square room. The tower is unusual, but a similar feature has been found in another house near Sounion, and there were square towers in the houses in Plate I.92 and Figure 25 below. Figure 22 seems much more regular, but notice the slope which governs this plan as in Figure 19. The section shows rooms at three levels and there is an extremely complex dog-leg staircase. ◆

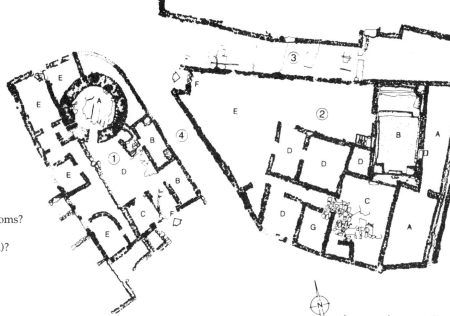

A: Tower with women's bedrooms?
B: Bedrooms?
C: Andron (men's dining room)?
D: Courtyard.
E: Entrance.
F: Milling chambers.
G: Washing table.
H: Courtyard.
I: Day room.
J: Bedrooms?
K: Washing room?

Figure 21   Thorikos. Plan of house and silver-washing complex in the industrial area illustrated in Plate I.93. Fifth century altered in the fourth century.

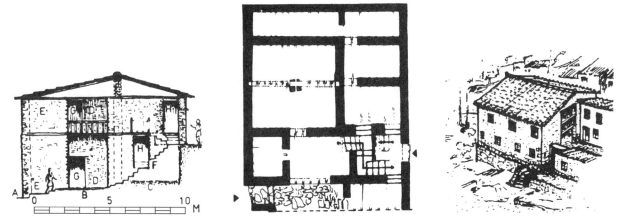

Figure 22   Thorikos, House No.1. Section, reconstructed ground plan and perspective view.

52

Rural housing

If it is no surprise that provincial urban housing is a bit like that in Athens, what about the rural settlements? After all, it is clear that agriculture was the basis of the Athenian economy in the fifth century, even if partial abandonment of the countryside was viable in time of war.

Look at Figures 23, 24 and 25 and Plate I.92. What can we learn from these about rural housing; and what are the difficulties in building up a picture from this evidence?

Discussion ———————————————————————

Figure 23 shows all the principal rural house sites in Attica known when the map was published in 1975. By any estimate this is a pitifully small sample, and emphasizes the extent to which archaeologists, over the last two centuries, have concentrated on the public buildings. Perhaps we have rather fallen for Thucydides' prophecy! Indeed from this sample we cannot really distinguish village homes from isolated farmsteads. Most rural housing was probably in village groups; and the house at Zoster, Figure 25, may well have been part of a seaside hamlet. On the other hand the Dema and Vari houses, Figure 24 and Plate I.92, were clearly isolated ones, yet they are not of a totally different type.

If you looked at the reconstructions and felt that they were much the same as the town houses, be careful, because all these reconstructions were drawn by one scholar, Dr John Ellis-Jones of Bangor, who makes the important caveat that they 'can have no claim to definitive accuracy but were intended to stimulate discussion'. We do know that houses in Attica were mostly of mud brick on stone foundations and usually, but not always, with tiled roofs. The foundation

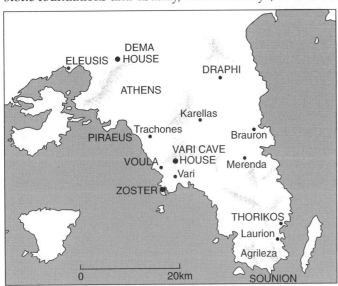

Figure 23   Map of Attica showing the location of principal excavated house sites, 1975.

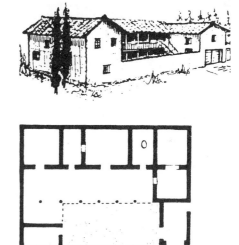

Figure 24   Ano Liosia, the 'Dema' House, 421–43. Reconstructed ground plan and perspective view.

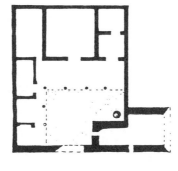

Figure 25   Zoster, The 'Priests' House', fifth century. Reconstructed ground floor plan as altered mid-fifth century, and perspective view.

widths give some indication of the number of storeys. But beyond that much is arguable.

The only big difference I notice between these rural houses and their urban counterparts is that they seem to have more space given to the court. This is hardly surprising; but it does emphasize the continuity of experience there would have been for the average Athenian even given a drift of population to the town. I think it is also interesting that the Vari and Dema houses are markedly similar in plan with their wide colonnade or verandah. Yet the Vari house is about a century later than the Dema house. It is probably contemporary with the House of the Greek Mosaics (Figure 20), and suggests that rural houses at least changed little, even though urban houses developed towards more regular planning. The Dema and Vari houses relate closely to a house type identified at Olynthos (Figure 14) where the courtyards have deep porticos (most easily seen in houses facing Street V in Figure 14). Yet the Olynthos houses are town buildings, so we should not see these Attic houses as a specifically rural type. Rather, it is further evidence that there was far less difference between rural and urban life in fifth-century Athens than in twentieth-century Britain. But to get a clearer picture you would need to look for clues in other sources such as Aristophanes or Thucydides. ◆

Now look back to the study guide at the beginning of Section 4 and see if you want to add anything to your notes on the three guiding questions I suggested.

4.2   Topic 2: Slavery

In Athens, slaves were property. According to Aristotle, in a seminal passage in the *Politics*, slaves were animate tools, superior to other tools in that they could obey or anticipate the will of the master. 'Property is a part of the household and the art of acquiring property is a part of the act of managing the household ... Now instruments are of various sorts; some are living, others lifeless ... and so a slave is a living possession and property a number of such instruments; and the servant is himself an instrument which takes precedence of all other instruments' (*Politics* 1, 1254, tr. J. Warrington, Dent, 1959).

Aristotle is, of course, referring to chattel slavery, which was the type practised in Athens and generally in the Mediterranean world. Although other forms of bondage and servitude did exist (for example, helots in Sparta), they are not relevant to our study of the material environment in Athens, where the existence of chattel slavery was an accepted aspect of 'how things were'. Here, we will be looking at the institution of slavery as one aspect of a functional analysis. Later, in Block 5, you will be looking at a few examples of writers who questioned some aspects of its justification, but so far as we know such questioning was largely confined to intellectuals and did not represent a general unease. (In the same part of the *Politics*, Aristotle says: 'Others affirm that the rule of a master over slaves is contrary to nature and that the distinction between slave and freeman exists by law only and not by nature; and being an interference with nature is therefore unjust.' The point was that slavery might be the fate of anyone, through the ill fortune of defeat in war, for example. Hence Greek experience denied that those who were slaves were so because they were slaves by nature. Nevertheless, the existence of slavery was a fact of life.)

The evidence concerning slavery at Athens is extremely varied. As always, we can look to the theory and practice of law for information about slaves as a status group. There is evidence from inscriptions, sometimes relating to manumission (i.e. release from slavery) but usually incidental to other matters, for example the listing of price and origin of slaves sold with other confiscated property in 415 (*ST* 17c); or details of the payments made to labourers working on the Erechtheion (*ST* 17f) – our extract names free men and *metics*, but slave craftsmen were also used. Slaves appear as minor characters in drama or are depicted on vases serving at symposia. (For symposium scenes, look at Illustration Booklet II.45–8.) The management of slaves is discussed in treatises on the *oikos* (?Aristotle) and on economic and political organization at Athens ([Xenophon] 1.10, *ST* 28) while in TV4 you can see a detailed study of the archaeological evidence relating to the silver mines at Laureion, the one extant example from our period of the large-scale systematic exploitation of slaves as a labour force apart. Notice, too, how in various written texts the vocabulary and concepts of slavery are used as terms of political abuse. Slavery was the opposite of freedom (see Old Oligarch, 1.8, 'For what the common people want is not to be slaves in a law-abiding city, but to be free and in control', *ST* 28).

I want to start by looking at the passages in *WA* which relate to slavery, and then move out to try to examine some of the questions which are raised directly or indirectly.

Please look up WA 4.1–11, 49 and 62–6, and consider:

1   *What was the contribution of slaves to the material environment?*

2   *Can we use evidence about slavery to shed light on other aspects of Athenian life and attitudes?*

Discussion

1   *What was the contribution of slaves to the material environment?*

The most important points are:

a)   *Numbers*. Estimates of population in the ancient world are notoriously unreliable, but if we accept that in 431 there were about twice as many slaves in Attica as there were adult male citizens, this gives a reasonable idea of proportions. It is also reasonable to assume that the proportion of slaves in Attica increased during the fifth century, responding to the demands for labour in building, mining and so on and perhaps acting as an index of the expectations and opportunities afforded by imperial expansion.

WA 4.63 claims that, in the fifth century, slaves were cheap to buy. Of course 'cheap' is relative. The reference to the 'drachma a day' craftsman's wage is misleading as an index of purchasing capacity, since such workers were not employed full-time by the state. Not only did they work as they pleased, the days of available employment might be at most 200 a year.

Consult Old Oligarch 1.10 (*ST* 28) for indirect evidence of the presence of slaves among the general population, plus evidence that they were not distinguished by dress.

b)   *Work done*. Mining seems to have been the exclusive preserve of slaves. Otherwise slaves were found in a range of crafts and trades, often working alongside citizens and masters, either on public buildings or in private industry (according to Xenophon, 'Those who can do so buy slaves to share their work with them', *Memorabilia*, 2.3.3). The contribution of slave labour to agriculture has been disputed by historians, but even in the absence of large-scale farming organization they probably still formed part of the work force of the *oikos* (see *WA* 4.50–2). (In Aristophanes' *Ecclesiazusae* 651, Praxagora automatically assumes that slaves will work the land.) The role of slaves within the *oikos* and in the public service was also important.

c)   *Slaves as a source of wealth*. Apart from the direct input of the slave to the *oikos* or workshop, a slave could be hired out to make money for the owner, either on an individual basis or as part of a gang. Some slaves working as individuals or groups may have lived apart from their owners. These were called the 'pay-bringers' or 'those living apart'. They could not contract their services for themselves: that had to be done by the owner. Some of the slaves may, however, have had a degree of independence. Aeschines, in a forensic speech (i.e. prepared for a law court) describes a group of leather-cutters leased out to a shop owner (*Against Timarchus* 47, 57). Each had to give his owner two obols per day but kept the rest of his wages, perhaps saving to purchase his freedom.

Sometimes large numbers were involved; look at *ST* 27(a) for evidence from Xenophon about the scale of Nikias' hiring-out operations. Lysias refers to the uncharacteristically large number of slaves (120) kept by his family, presumably to work their arms factory (*Against Eratosthenes* 19, *ST* 20).

Further comment

The sources relevant to the organization of supply of slaves are rather meagre, but a substantial trade must have existed, given the numbers involved. Import from Scythia and other Black Sea areas is attested for Athens and Laureion (TV4 discussed the evidence from tombstones on the origin of slaves). Herodotus (5.6) says that Thracians sold their children for export and Thucydides (6.62 and 7.13) recounts how the Athenians sold the entire population of Hyccara in Sicily for 120 talents.

2 Can we use evidence about slavery to shed light on other aspects of Athenian life and attitudes?

As always, we can't simply cut off the material environment from other aspects of Athenian life. For example:

a) Did the widespread existence of slavery result in fear among the citizen population?

b) Did the existence of slavery contribute to (or derive from) a pattern of social and racial attitudes?

c) To what extent was the democracy dependent on slavery?

Considering these questions in order:

a) *Fear.* (In fact the institution of slavery resulted in a network of fears, not all one way.)

The Old Oligarch perhaps provides evidence of absence of fear rather than the reverse (1.10), although we do not need to accept literally his view of the licence allowed to slaves in the city. Certainly there is no evidence of organized slave revolts, although no doubt slaves ran away if the opportunity arose, as the often quoted example from Thucydides suggests (7.27). The absconding slaves did not win freedom; they were just sold on by the Spartans.

However, there is some evidence from Greece generally to suggest that the support of slave populations could be exploited for political reasons. Manumission or, in rare cases, citizenship might be promised in return for support during war or *stasis* (for example, Thucydides 3.73). Conversely, alliance between *poleis* might specifically include agreement not to tamper with dependent labour – for example, after 421 the Athenian treaty with Sparta included provision that 'In case of a rising of the [Spartan] slaves [i.e. helots] the Athenians are to come to the aid of Sparta with all their strength, according to their resources' (Thucydides 5.23 and cf. 4.80). In contrast to the helots at Sparta who were not only in a majority but were concentrated in social groups and worked all the land, the Athenian system of dispersed chattel slavery made Athenians much less vulnerable to uprising, as opposed to desertion.

The Athenian legal system formally recognized fear by the requirement that evidence from slaves be extracted under torture, the point being that a greater fear must be induced than the fear that the slave already had for the owner. A late-fourth-century source (Ps. Arist. Oec. 1344 and 35) assumes that the life of the slave consisted of work, punishment and food, and a speech of Demosthenes (8.51) asserts that while free men are deterred from wrong-doing by fear of *shame*, slaves are deterred only by *fear of bodily pain*. Fear of being enslaved was very real in time of war or political dependence and could strike all sections of society, though it was the normal fate of the women and children (for example, Euripides, *The Women of Troy*, discussed in Section 8). Evidence from forensic oratory suggests that slaves who were free-born Hellenes had a claim on better treatment (Demosthenes 19.196–8, Aeschines 2.5).

b) *Social attitudes*

Because the Athenian citizenship was so exclusive, there was limited social mobility following manumission. The possibility of manumission, either from direct act of the owner or more commonly by purchase, existed for domestic and workshop slaves, but on manumission they became *metics*, not citizens. Of course the fact that some slaves obtained their freedom did not affect the institution as such.

It was the custom not to enslave Athenians at Athens, Corinthians at Corinth, etc., and as we saw above many slaves at Athens were non-Greek. In discussing the theoretical basis of slavery, Aristotle makes much of the fact that

> Hellenes do not like to call Hellenes slaves but confine the term to barbarians ... Hellenes regard themselves as noble everywhere, and not only in their own country, but they deem the barbarians noble only when at home, thereby implying that there are two sorts of nobility and freedom, the one absolute, the other relative.

> (*Politics*, 1255A–B)

Of course Aristotle was writing much later and with a different purpose in mind, and it will no doubt have occurred to you that there is plenty of evidence in Thucydides of the readiness of the Athenians to sell into slavery Greeks who attempted to revolt from the Empire. However, the fact that large supplies of slaves for the more menial occupations tended to be brought from certain areas, such as the Black Sea, may have led to a conventional identification of slavery or slavish attitudes with geographical origin. (Compare the way Aristophanes insults Kleon in the *Knights* by identifying him with the Paphlagonian slave (*ST* 5b).)

The idea of being a dependent labourer was inimical to even poor citizens. The poor citizen kept self- and public respect by being an independent labourer. There was apparently no stigma attached to physical work as such by poorer citizens; it was being employed by or subject to another man which was disgraceful. Thus, in a sense, the existence of dependent labour boosted by comparison the social status of poor citizens. Manual work was, however, despised by the upper class and intellectual writers on the grounds that it dissipated energy and time which should be spent on civic matters. Consider, for example, Aristotle when referring to an ideal state of affairs:

> the citizens must not lead the life of mechanics or tradesmen, for such a life is ignoble and inimical to virtue. Neither must they be husbandmen since leisure is necessary both for the development of virtue and the performance of political duties.

> (*Politics* 1328)

Of course, the point about the ideal states proposed by most of the philosophers is that citizenship is restricted to the propertied classes.

c) *Dependence on slavery*

This brings us to the relationship between the institution of slavery and the existence and prosperity of the democracy. (A broader question, 'Was Greek civilization based on slave labour?', has been explored by M.I. Finley. The most accessible reference is probably Chapter 6 of *Economy and Society in Ancient Greece*, Pelican, 1983.) In one sense, such questions are meaningless: slavery existed and we have no evidence on which to speculate about what Athenian society would have been like without it. But in another sense, tracing the relationship between the institution of slavery and the practices and values associated with the exploitation of natural resources, trade, industry and leisure, public order, tactical moves in time of war, and above all citizenship, can help us illuminate key features and points of difficulty, change and tension. I am not going to take this question further at the moment but keep it in mind as you look back at this half of the block and as you work through the next half (especially Section 6). ◆

Further reading: M.I. Finley (1980), *Ancient Slavery and Modern Ideology*, Chatto and Windus.

This explores aspects of the moral tensions felt by twentieth-century students when dealing with slavery. On the one hand, we may find it hard to look at the ancient evidence independently of our perceptions of the forms of slavery practised in modern societies with their attendant horrors. On the other hand, the fact that the ancient evidence tends not to be concerned with brutality and exploitation should not make us think ancient slavery was a 'sanitized' institution. The point is that ancient society not only accepted but *assumed* slavery, and that exploited people left little or no direct evidence of their feelings or individuality.

Now look back to the study guide at the beginning of Section 4 and see if you want to add anything to your notes on the three guiding questions I suggested.

4.3 Topic 3: Wealth

One of the dichotomies drawn rather crudely by the Old Oligarch in his pamphlet is between rich and poor. Given the political slant of his analysis and his desire to portray the ordinary people (the mob in his formulation) in the worst possible light, and given that a real situation hardly ever shows itself in such conveniently clear-cut terms, we might reformulate this as a contrast between rich*er* and poor*er* (citizens). One thing about which he complains seems to point to some sort of redistribution of wealth:

> ... where it is a matter of providing choral or dramatic festivals or athletic contests or of equipping a trireme, it is the rich who put up the money while the common people enjoy their festivals and contests and are provided with their triremes. Whether it is taking part in the different kinds of festivals and contests or serving in the fleet, the common people constantly expects to receive money, so that its own wealth may grow and the rich may become poorer.

(*ST* 28, I.13)

The passage suggests indirect information about attitudes – that personal wealth was both desirable and could be a source of envy and that its use was a proper subject for public display.

In this section we shall be trying to discover what the Athenians understood by personal wealth and how it was obtained. This leads to further questions about what the possession of wealth achieved for the holder, how it was regarded in different sections of society and how attitudes to wealth influenced and were affected by changes in Athens in the fifth century. Some of these questions will spill over into other sections of this block and, as with slavery, it will be clear that there are few issues that can be neatly confined to the material environment only.

There is no systematic treatment of wealth in WA*, so I suggest you start by looking up the small number of references in the Index, noting down information which seems to you to be relevant to the themes I outlined in the preceding paragraph. In the discussion I will concentrate on private wealth, leaving public wealth for consideration in the next section. (Just bear in mind that the Athenians had public wealth based on fees and dues from Piraeus and leases from the silver mines as well as the benefits of empire.)*

Discussion _____

The most important general points to be gleaned from *WA* are:

a) Wealth was initially based on property. Originally it was measured agriculturally (see *WA* 4.7 on the citizen census classes).

b) During the fifth century other sources of wealth became significant. For example, this is shown by the importance attached to Piraeus as a trading centre and by the general increase in prosperity evidenced by the rise in numbers in the hoplite class.

c) Personal wealth was important as a necessary basis for independence, enabling men to fulfil civic and military responsibilities and to make a public reputation.

d) There is evidence that the general increase in prosperity and broadening of the basis of wealth brought its own problems. *WA* mentions (H.I.37) the evidence from Aristophanes about comic exploitation (perhaps as a political weapon) of snobbish attitudes to the sources of wealth. A late source, Xenophon in *Memorabilia*, 3.11.4 (you can look it up in *WA* 4.38), yields indirect evidence about the sources of wealth considered acceptable. However, the gloss supplied here by the authors of *WA* about the chief sources of wealth is somewhat misleading, especially given the nature of the source. Clearly we need to look at a much broader range of evidence in order to understand what was happening. In the paragraphs which follow, I shall refer extensively to the work of J.K. Davies in *Athenian Propertied Families* (Oxford, 1971) and (especially) *Wealth and the Power of Wealth in Classical Athens* (Arno Press, 1981). ◆

4.3.1 A working definition of private wealth – the liturgical class

One way of approaching the problem of definition is to identify a group who under Athenian criteria were clearly regarded as possessing wealth. J.K. Davies has suggested a means of identifying those who were not only sufficiently well off to be at leisure (i.e. they did not have to earn their daily living) but also had the *conspicuous* wealth which enabled them to perform liturgies (i.e. the *plousioi* referred to by the Old Oligarch). The numbers liable for military liturgies (for example, the trierarchy) can be estimated from the numbers of ships available in any one year. For example, Herodotus says that in 480 the Athenian fleet amounted to 180 (Herodotus 8.1, 8.14, 8.41), counting both Artemision and Salamis. In 431 the Athenians had just over 300 ships (Thucydides 2.13.8). The Old Oligarch (3.4), probably referring to the 420s, says '400 trierarchs are appointed each year'. Allowing for the fact that one individual did not actually undertake more than one liturgy in a year, about 300 seems a minimum estimate of the numbers who could afford the trierarchy in any one year. Since it was unlikely anyone would be a trierarch in two successive years, the total number of eligible rich must have been higher, although it is likely to have diminished towards the end of the fifth century. There is some evidence (for example, from Lysias) that after about 412 the trierarchy could be shared (i.e. some liturgists had become financially worse off and/or more were needed). Evidence about the numbers who could afford the festival liturgies such as the *choregia* is somewhat complicated but indicates that in the early fourth century probably approaching 300 were eligible. The corresponding figures for the fifth century are not known but would probably have been higher. Remember, too, that those who were well off but not sufficiently wealthy to be liturgists still had to perform their military obligations, providing their own equipment for cavalry or hoplite service.

4.3.2 Sources of wealth

Agricultural property was the traditional source of wealth. However, there is plenty of evidence to show that in the course of the fifth century there were significant new sources of personal wealth which, unlike agricultural wealth, were not based on inheritance and the inalienability of land. The most important new sources of wealth are suggested by Davies (*Wealth and the Power of Wealth*, Chapter 4).

a) *Industrial slavery*

For the basis and extent of this, see notes to TV4 in the TV Notes and Section 4.2 above on slavery. Neutron analysis of silver, used for coinage, suggests Laureion was in use to some extent from the 520s. The requirement for large numbers of slave miners and their regular replacement ensured a good return for large investors. It may even be that the use of large-scale industrial slavery was unique to the Athenians.

b) *Rents*

Rents from houses and farmland are mentioned in inscriptions and written sources. There was demand from *metics*, who were not allowed to own houses and land, and tended to concentrate in or near Athens and Piraeus (see Section 6 below).

Empire brought visitors and merchants, and from the 420s the exigencies of wartime evacuation and urbanization increased demand for rented property. The sources point to multiple occupancy (compare *ST* 28, Old Oligarch 1.17, and Aristophanes' *Knights*, 792–3, *ST* 5(b)). Excavation has revealed that, in the fifth century, building took place in and around Athens on previously agricultural sites.

c) *Property outside Attica*

This could include land occupied by Athenians in Athenian colonies, land owned by an Athenian god or goddess and leased out to Athenian citizens, and land assigned to Athenian citizens in cleruchies (see *WA* 5.91) as well as property privately owned. Note that the aims of cleruchies included settling lower-class citizens, so the benefits of land outside Attica were not necessarily confined to the wealthy class. Note also that fourth-century evidence suggests that one of the principal causes of resentment of the Athenian Empire was the financial exploitation of the subject states. An example of the evidence concerning property held outside Attica is to be found in the *stele* recording the confiscations of 415. Land in three parts of Euboia belonging to Oionias was sold for 81 talents, an enormous sum (1G $1^3$422 lines 375–8).

d) *Risk capital lent at interest*

Examples are to be found in maritime loans (bottomry), other loans and banking. Such activities were an important aspect of *metic* activity (although citizens are also to be found). Banking yields the rare examples of *metics* attaining citizenship (and even becoming members of the liturgical class). That a wealthy *metic* banker could obtain the necessary political support to ensure a special grant of citizenship perhaps indicates something of the special relationship between wealth and politics.

e) *Financial gains from politics, bribes, booty*

This is well attested from the fourth century but we lack direct evidence from the fifth century, although Themistokles' career was supposed to have been profitable. Compare Old Oligarch III.3 (*ST* 28) who asserts that the transactions of politics are facilitated by money.

4.3.3 Wealth and social mobility

At the beginning of the fifth century most wealth was concentrated largely in the hands of a few propertied families who were also politically prominent. As the democracy and the empire developed and new sources of wealth emerged, wealth continued to be important as a basis for political activity, ensuring the necessary leisure and helping build the necessary reputation of honour and success.

The relationship between wealth, expenditure and political influence under the full democracy is an interesting and complex one. We shall consider in other sections various ways in which ordinary citizens attained at least some of the leisure and financial security to enable them to participate in politics, and the ways in which the fruits of empire made this easier. As we saw above, the advantages of empire certainly did not bypass the propertied class. Nevertheless, in the fifth century great wealth was not a *direct* political lever to the extent that it had been earlier or was to be in the fourth century, when the *polis* was more dependent on the wealth of individuals to meet public expenditure and the interests of an impoverished propertied class might then be of more direct account. In the fifth century the conspicuous display of wealth had to be seen to combine regard for the reputation of the wealthy man with the use of his money for the public good. We see this brought out in the speeches produced by Lysias, where his wealthy defendants boast of the public benefits they have financed and urge this as grounds for acquittal (compare also the 'model' speech by Antiphon the Orator (*ST* 3(a)). That such pleading was thought likely to appeal to the jury tells us a good deal about Athenian attitudes to wealth.

Nevertheless, attitudes to the newly wealthy seem to have been ambivalent. Old Comedy and the anti-democratic writers make much of the allegedly humble origins of men like Kleon. (In fact, Kleon's father was a festival liturgist.) But the real point is that these men did not come from the traditionally political aristocratic families, and that they used their wealth as a foundation for the acquisition and exercise of the political skills necessary from the mid-fifth century on. This meant, among other things, engaging the support of the *demos*. It is interesting that Nikias, another 'new' man, seems to be counted as an honorary *kaloskagathos* (the term of commendation used to praise a 'fine gentleman'). Even Thucydides goes out of his way to praise his character (7.86). But of course, Nikias sided with the traditionalists and moderate democrats. *That*, not birth or wealth, is the contrast between him and Kleon, and that is what governs the way the two men are presented to us by the written sources. The adjustment of attitudes to keep pace with the facts of social mobility usually takes some time, and by the end of the fifth century, as we would expect, there is evidence that the children or grandchildren of the newly prominent inter-marry with the children of the aristocratic families.

In this section, I have deliberately talked about private wealth – its sources, the way it was used and attitudes to it – and not about abstractions such as 'the economy', which for the Athenians had neither the conceptual significance nor autonomous status which we assume today. Wealth, like slavery, is just one among the elements which coalesced to set the framework within which the Athenians lived, but which also enables us to confront the ways in which they thought. In this section we have concentrated on the most wealthy, but have also touched on evidence for an increase in general prosperity and the ways in which this was achieved and disseminated through the citizen body. In the next section we can look in more detail at one aspect of this, the gains derived from empire.

Before reading further, please go back to the study guide at the beginning of Section 4 and review the progress of your notes in response to the three guiding questions I suggested.

4.4 Topic 4: The benefits of empire

The title for this section is very much a shorthand one. We are dealing with a period running from the institution of the naval league in the 470s down to the end of the Athenian Empire at the end of the century. Just as the League and Empire changed and developed (and contracted!), so did the benefits. You may remember that at the end of Block 3 (Section 8.4) we considered briefly the attitudes to the Athenian Empire held in the allied and subject states and the way in which these states were treated by Athens. Here we shall focus on the other side of the coin and look at the internal effects of empire on Athens.

Please now read WA *Sections 5.84–5.91. You do not need to make extensive notes but jot down a response to these questions:*

1   *What material benefits came to the Athenians as a result of empire? To what extent can we identify individuals or groups who benefited? Do other points occur to you which are not mentioned here?*

2   *The authors of* WA *subscribe to a particular interpretation of the benefits of empire. Can you summarize it? Does this view seem justified by the evidence you have studied?*

(The discussion will aim to build on what you gain from WA *and to introduce an alternative perspective.)*

Discussion _____

1   Benefits

WA mentions ships (initially) replaced by cash tribute, indemnities etc. and the official posts associated with the bureaucracy of empire. There were also opportunities to acquire land holdings outside Attica, either by purchase of real estate (see Section 4.3.2 above) or by settlement as cleruchs or colonists (for an example, see the inscription referring to Brea, *WA* 5.91). Trade and industry at Athens were stimulated and the grain supply safeguarded.

The examples given affect a broad spread of the Athenian community. Note that the number of official posts was large and that opportunities for the acquisition of land, although different in *kind*, existed for lower census groups as well as the rich. The stimulation of industrial and building activities in Athens and the importance of Piraeus meant that citizens of other *poleis* were attracted and enriched.

Other points which may have occurred to you are the benefits brought in by visitors, who had to come to deliver tribute or to accept the jurisdiction of the Athenian courts in important matters (where severe penalties might be involved). Also, where the balance of tribute exceeded immediate military and naval requirements, public decisions had to be made about its use (see below). Remember, too, that immediate material benefits inevitably have effects of their own. Money raised from tribute does not have to be raised from the Athenian rich, attendance in the courts keeps the jurors busy and remunerated, a plurality of official posts gives a broad section of people a stake in the Empire. All these factors thus affect political relationships *within* Athens.

2   WA's interpretation

The *WA* authors make a definite judgement: 'The real beneficiaries of the empire, though, were the Athenian poor, especially the *thetes*' (5.91). The evidence put forward to support this assertion seems to be based on the role of the fleet in employing rowers and securing the grain supply. Of course, the latter is vital, the breakdown of the arrangements resulted in starvation and defeat (for *everyone*) in 404. So far as the fleet is concerned, *metics* and slaves played a part too, and Thucydides refers to the dangers of a shortage of hired rowers; so I do not think it is safe to assume that there was a surplus of potentially discontented *thetes* who could only be absorbed in the fleet. The arrangements for colonies and cleruchies indicate that broader benefits were also attractive to the lower census groups. The authors of *WA* seem to be much influenced by the comments on empire and the *demos* to be found in texts such as the Old Oligarch (I.14–18, *ST* 28) and the Aristotelian *Constitution of Athens* (24–5, *ST* 6).

Please look at these passages now.

These are, of course, important sources, but they do not tell the whole story. The Old Oligarch's basic viewpoint is that the democracy was parasitic on the Empire. The Aristotelian account, written much later, appears to be more factual, but its purpose is to explain how the demos gained a living, as the opening sentence of 25 makes clear. ◆

In the next part of this section, I am going to explore some aspects of a contrasting argument – that the benefits of empire were in fact dispersed through the Athenian citizen community and reflected a broader identity of interest which, although subject to tensions, did not break down until the Empire was shattered by defeat in the Peloponnesian War. One way of approaching this is to itemize the material benefits of empire and decide whether they were primarily or exclusively directed at one section of the citizen community.

1   Financial

In addition to the tribute, we can cite the fees and dues arising from control of trade, harbour rights in Piraeus, etc. (Of course, it is impossible to be precise about the extent to which Piraeus would still have been a centre for trade and prosperity had the Empire not existed. In the fourth century it was still an important centre – whether as a result of primarily geographical or primarily historical momentum is impossible to say.)

You read in Section 2 of this block something of the argument about the extent to which the Periclean building programme redistributed imperial tribute in the direction of the working citizens. Plutarch suggested there was a conflict between the policy of Pericles and that of his opponent in the 440s – Thucydides, son of Melesias, who had succeeded Kimon as the leader of the aristocratic faction (Plutarch, *Pericles*, *passim*). According to Plutarch, Pericles proposed using surplus tribute for the building programme, while Thucydides wanted it retained for its original purpose. An interesting parallel is to be found in the earlier debate about whether to distribute Laureion surplus to the citizens or to follow Themistokles' advice to build a fleet: Herodotus 7.144, *ST* 13(h).

We do not know the facts of the dispute or why Thucydides was ostracized, but Plutarch goes on to suggest that one of the aims of the Periclean building programme was to provide employment for the potentially disruptive urban *demos*. Now as you have already seen from the Erechtheion accounts (*ST* 17(f)), it was not the case that only citizen labour was employed, and anyway citizens did not work full-time. It is also doubtful whether lack of employment made Greeks disruptive. Lack of grain might do so, or lack of land or political rights. It seems much more likely that Plutarch (writing in the early second century CE) was led astray by the urban conditions prevailing during the early Roman Empire and anachronistically imputed similar public order concerns to the Greeks. (A. Andrews, 'The opposition to Pericles', *Journal of Hellenic Studies*, 1978, pp.1–8, goes into the whole question in detail.)

It is then safer to say that the financial benefits of empire were not 'creamed off' and directed *only* towards the urban poor in their capacity as building workers or rowers in the fleet. However, this is not to say that poorer citizens did not benefit, either directly from pay for civic and military service and public works, or indirectly because of a more buoyant economic climate. This inevitably had political results since, once the *polis* took on a major role as a source of income, the dependence of poorer citizens on the patronage of the rich was lessened. To find a satisfactory answer to the question about social spread of financial benefits, we would need to know the backgrounds of those who became imperial officials (the sources do not tell us). We would also need to consider the effect of the relief of financial and tax pressures from the richer citizens (there is no direct evidence, but we can speculate). In Part 2 of this block you will be looking in detail at the Funeral Speech of Pericles in Thucydides Bk.2, where the benefits of empire for the citizens as a group are praised. You will probably want to add to your notes on this topic when you have studied Sections 5 and 6.

2   Land

Settlement outside Attica began very early with Eion and Skyros in *c*.475 and trading posts and mines confiscated from Thasos in 463–2 (Thucydides 1.100–101). In the case of Thasos, Athenians took the income from the mine leases. In the case of colonies and cleruchies, poorer citizens could benefit and the rich could acquire real estate. It does not seem justified, therefore, to assert that it was only or even primarily the poor who benefited.

3 Social and political benefits

Not all benefits are tangible, and those that are have knock-on effects. In Section 6 you will be looking at ways in which relative prosperity and leisure went together as the basis for civic participation in the developed democracy.

Given the stress on competition and reputation in Athenian social values, and the consequent scope for envy and jealousy, we would expect to see evidence of discord if the benefits of the Empire were filtered exclusively towards one section of the community. Therefore we need to ask: if the Athenian Empire benefited the poorer citizens so much (and it did, although not exclusively them), why did the upper classes support it? The first step to answering this is to gauge the extent to which they did in fact support it. We know that aristocrats like Kimon in fact developed the Empire, but did his successors support it if it merely fed the aspirations of the *demos*?

One possible answer is to be found in Thucydides 8.48 – where the historian records the debates preceding the oligarchic coup of 411. In speaking against a plan to recall Alcibiades and end the democracy, Phrynichus (whose acuteness of judgement is generally praised by Thucydides) claims that such a move would not be popular among the revolting cities of the Empire since 'they saw no reason to suppose that they would be any better off under the so-called upper classes themselves'. Significantly when the oligarchs eventually took power they wanted initially to negotiate peace with Sparta while still retaining the Empire. Such arguments suggest that, while the upper classes certainly did benefit financially by obtaining land and avoiding crippling demands for liturgies, they received political benefits too. I do not think the political benefits were only of a negative kind (such as avoiding excessive envy from the poorer citizens because these too had their own opportunities). It seems clear that the political benefits were positive. Empire brought the prestige associated with the senior political and military posts, still largely the province of the upper classes even in the developed democracy, and the opportunity to develop and exercise political skills. If the taking and holding of empire involved an alliance between the body of citizens and the ambitious grandees, then of course we should expect to see the alliance falling apart as Athens tottered to defeat. And you already know that this is what happened.

I have not attempted to give a full treatment of the many problems associated with defining the benefits derived from empire, nor with trying to identify the recipients, but I hope I have opened up enough issues to suggest that the first sentence of WA 5.91 is an over-simplification. In suggesting an alternative way of approaching this issue, I have anticipated some topics which we will be considering later in this block. You will therefore need to add to your notes later on, and then to decide your own conclusions. In the Revision Block (Block 6) there will be an opportunity to draw together the threads of your study of Athenian imperialism, both inside and outside Attica.

As usual at the end of a topic, please look back to the guiding questions I suggested in the study guide at the beginning of Section 4 and update your notes.

4.5 Topic 5: The effects of war on the Athenians

War was endemic in Greece. In assessing its impact on Athens, our problem is to distinguish between, on the one hand, the essential features of a society which had to be structured and organized to cope with a virtually annual expectation of war and, on the other hand, tensions and changes which resulted from or contributed to unusual or severe aspects of the impact of war.

In a sense, we are asking: what 'normal' effects of war could the Athenians absorb? At what point, if at all, were their institutions, social organization and values challenged by it?

Your set reading is taken from *WA* Chapter 6 and Thucydides 2.13–17.

At this point, please turn to WA Chapter 6. You will need to study 6.1–20 and also look at 6.25 and the first paragraph of 6.26. The rest of the chapter, which deals with technical detail and fourth-century developments, is optional reading. As you read through 6.1–20 and 25–6, look for information which will help you identify possible points of stress in Athenian society as it responded to wars in the fifth century. Bear in mind, too, what you learnt about the Persian Wars in Block 1.

Discussion

You may well have picked out different points from mine. There is no single 'correct' response. The important thing is to be able to *justify* your selection and to be able to distinguish key points from minor issues.

1   Because war was endemic (*WA* 6.2) there seems to have been no pacifist party. Pacificism would have entailed acceptance not merely of defeat but of *slavery*. However, this fact should not blind us to matters of disagreement about the fighting or direction of particular campaigns. If war between states is an accepted political tool, war policy becomes an essential feature of political debate. If the consequences of defeat are traumatic, then the role of negotiation is vital. Furthermore, the avoidance of defeat may seem more important than the winning of victory. Yet in a society where war is seen as *instrumental* (a means of achieving honour, reputation, booty, land), the aim of merely avoiding defeat may bring its own political problems (see also *WA* 6.15).

Figure 26   Attic red figure kylix from Vulci, Etruria. Achilles and Patroklos, by the Sosias painter, *c*.500 (diameter of field 17.5cm., 6.5in.) (Cat.2278; ARV 21.1).

2   The absence of standing armies (*WA* 6.2) means that the ability to wage war is an important attribute of all male citizens. It also means that the campaigning season, however short, has important implications – for example, for the proper practice of agriculture (see *WA* 1.11–12: seed time and harvest wait for no one). In a citizen army, the effects of success and defeat are immediately and widely felt. There can be no concealment.

3   The stress on religious ritual (*WA* 6.3) involves special obligation towards a city's gods who must be kept benevolent. Lack of respect to the gods might challenge their benevolence. Defeat for a city could also mean defeat for its gods.

4   Major campaigns or prolonged war strained natural resources (*WA* 6.4) and logistics. Careful planning was essential and sea-power vital to a *polis* lacking essential items. Athens had special problems because she was not self-sufficient in food (*WA* 6.8 and see also *WA* 5.74). Note the role of the Empire in meeting the costs. Just as in previous centuries the development of hoplite warfare (to replace individual combat) had been closely related to social and political changes, so in the fifth century the development of large-scale naval power was both the cause and effect of changes in the balance of political power and outlook in Athens.

5   The drain on human life, directly and indirectly, was great. *WA* 6.10 perhaps underrates the effect of *prolonged* conflict as experienced in the Peloponnesian War. As well as losses in hand-to-hand fighting and skirmishing, we have to add those drowned at sea or dying from disease or wounds or starvation – both on campaigns (look again at Thucydides 7.87) and in Attica (see Xenophon, *Hellenica* 2 *ST* 27(b)). (For an example from the Pentekontaëtia, see the casualty list of the Erechtheid tribe 460 or 459, *ST* 17(d).) There is ample evidence in both Thucydides and Xenophon of severe shortages of fighting and rowing manpower towards the end of the Peloponnesian War.

6   The large-scale challenges of the Persian and Peloponnesian Wars seem to have brought adaptation in both organization and fighting techniques. The Persian Wars developed the role of the *strategos*, led to the enlargement of the fleet and provided the political justification for empire. The Peloponnesian War led perhaps to an increasing professionalism as shown in the fourth-century separation of military and political leadership (*WA* 6.25) and the emergence of new ways of recruiting troops. The use of mercenaries was bound to increase in the fourth century, given that the citizen army had shown itself unable to fight prolonged and distant campaigns and also meet civic and agricultural obligations at home.

7   The impact of the Peloponnesian War is in one sense unique because it involved a massive defeat for the Athenians. Not only did they lose their fleet, but the government of the *polis* collapsed. *Stasis* intensified. In contrast to the first Persian invasion, the Athenians in 404 could not fully evacuate the city. Worst of all, they lost the Empire. Defeat was therefore, total. ◆

Now read Thucydides 2.13–17 (Athens in 431; the evacuation of Attica). You have already encountered parts of this extract. Here, I want you to go through it again, noting down points which add a detailed perspective to the general features we abstracted from your WA reading.

Discussion

2.13   Archidamos' invasion took the route along a line between Eleusis and Acharnai (you can locate this on Course Guide Map 5). We will be looking in more detail at the significance of these places in Part 2 of this block. Note the essentially defensive policy of Pericles. Because the city itself was so well defended (see Course Guide Map 6) and the Athenians so rich in resources, Pericles thought that by evacuating Attica the Athenians could wait for the Spartans to exhaust themselves and their resources. Remember, however, that Pericles was defensive by *land* because of Spartan expertise, but aggressive by sea, because the Athenians' strength was based on the fleet. Compare *WA* 6.8 on the general Greek fear of ravaging, and contrast the effect on the Athenians (psychologically as well as materially) of the prolonged Spartan occupation of parts of Attica in the later years of the war. We can see here a potential disagreement about the conduct of the war. (Also compare Thucydides 2.55–65.)

2.14   Thucydides emphasizes the effect on rural people of moving into the city. Stock was sent to the islands, but (in contrast to the Persian Wars) families to Athens. Note the inference that timber was so valuable it was stripped from the houses. Remember that some land could still have been worked if within daily walking distance and considered safe from ravaging.

2.15   An apparent digression on the way in which Theseus reconciled the agricultural base of Attica with the *synoecism*, concentration of government in the city. However, when taken with the information in the next chapter, Thucydides may be hinting that the evacuation of Attica was justified in public propaganda by appeal to the example of the mythological/heroic king.

2.16   Builds on the preceding section by emphasizing the cults and temples of Athens, but note especially the tension implicit in the second paragraph of this section, which deals with the sustained rural and local identity of 'most Athenians'. Thucydides draws our attention to their reluctance to leave their *homes* and *temples*: 'they prepared to change their whole way of life, leaving behind them what each man regarded as his own city [*polis*]'. Note the evidence for public concern about religious orthodoxy in times of disaster *and* the persistence of the effects of the Persian invasion, both agriculturally and psychologically.

2.17   Here Thucydides hints at some of the practical and psychological difficulties of the large increase in the number of people in the city (see Aristophanes, *ST* 5(b), *Knights* 792–3). Elsewhere he records the traumatic effects of the plague, which were doubtless made worse by overcrowding (Thucydides 2.47–55). For the economic effects of demand for housing, refer back to Section 4.3.2 of this block.

Thus, as so often, a close reading of Thucydides signposts a way forward by suggesting particular examples of issues which both he and our other sources consider more broadly in the context of the later development of the war. The passage we have just studied is particularly valuable in conveying a vivid and immediate sense of the impact of enforced urbanization and crowding. As you work through Part 2 of this block, look for the political effects of this: for example, loss of some agricultural land and therefore increased reliance on the fleet to safeguard food supplies; tension between rural and urban interests; intensification of the political temperature; the fact that attendance at the Assembly was now more accessible (except to those away in the forces). If the 'defensive' policy did not work, dissent was easily expressed. Note, too, how Thucydides' account shows the importance of *place* in the Athenian outlook. Removal from the land was not only removal from the ancestral *oikos* but from the cults and temples associated with that place. We might compare the importance of 'place' in the wider sense in determining civic status. If a man moved from his own *polis*, he became a *metic*. Slavery, too, was a forcible sign that men, women and children, including Greeks, had lost their own roots, their place, and become chattels. ◆

Keep these general and particular features of the impact of war in mind as you work through Part 2 of this block. In Part 2, we shall be looking at a number of sources and topics concerned with stability, tension and change in the social and political structure and the values associated with it, while in Block 5 you will be considering problems of change and innovation in philosophy and religion. As always, you will need to distinguish between short-term and long-term change. It is a truism that war challenges existing structures and exposes weakness. We have to decide whether these challenges are temporary or more penetrating. Do the pre-existing structures and patterns return, or can war sometimes also act as a catalyst for change? The situation for the Greeks is particularly complicated to assess since war was an essential and expected part of their social, political and religious structures and values. These structures were thus already adapted for war. The degree to which they were nevertheless stressed is therefore highly instructive. We shall have to decide the extent to which the stresses were the result of war. We shall gather together these themes in the Revision Block, but you will find it helpful to add to your notes during the rest of Block 4 and in Block 5 by referring back to the suggestions for the assessment of change in the introduction to this block.

Please look again at the guiding questions in the study guide at the beginning of Section 4 and update your notes with respect to this topic

PART 2   THE ATHENIAN ETHOS

INTRODUCTION TO PART 2

The first part of the block was concerned with the material environment. We studied this by looking at what the Athenians built and made, how they organized their surroundings and how they used and adapted the 'constants' of land, climate and war. But it was apparent as we worked that we could not make a rigid division between 'material' and 'mental'. To understand what they made, we had to think about why they made it and how it was used; and to understand how they adapted the way they lived in response to natural and human pressures, we had to think about their assumptions and the implicit and explicit attitudes they adopted.

I am going to take this one step further in this second part of the block (four weeks' work – see the study guide on p.6). We have called this part the Athenian *ethos*. This entails analysing how the Athenians saw themselves in relation to their environment and how they perceived, interpreted and debated this relationship. Because this emphasizes verbal expression, we will be more concerned with written texts – the Funeral Speech in Thucydides (Section 5); *Crito*, a short dialogue by Plato (Section 7); and *The Women of Troy*, a play by Euripides (Section 8). The sources we will use in Section 6 are more diffuse, since there we will be concerned with the Athenians' rationale for their social and political organization and the way in which they tackled the relationships between values and the demands of circumstance.

So in order to relate our study to the theme of tensions and change, we will need to keep in mind broad questions such as:

> Did the Athenians have a clear and unified picture of themselves?
> What sort of issues, activities and values did they agree about?
> What did they disagree about?
> Did they 'agree to disagree', or is there evidence of challenge and change? If there was challenge and change, how deep did these go?

As before, we have chosen texts which are enjoyable and valuable in themselves, as well as for the evidence they yield on the overall themes of the block. We have selected the Funeral Speech in Thucydides as the touchstone for the issues explored in the block and, in my discussion at the end of Section 5, I have suggested some specific questions and themes which will help you to relate the different sections of the block to one another (with reminders at the end of each section). However, each section is self-contained and you can, if you prefer, work through each individually, leaving your work on integration until the end of the block.

5 THE FUNERAL SPEECH (THUCYDIDES 2.34–46)

Study guide

For this section you will need your Thucydides text, *WA*, the *ST* booklet and The Offprints.

> The Funeral Speech put into the mouth of Pericles, Athens' most famous statesman, by the historian Thucydides is the most famous statement of what made Athens great.
>
> (*WA* p.56)

The first part of this sentence is accurate, but of course the fact that Thucydides attributes the speech to Pericles brings us back into the problems of interpretation and intention which we considered in Block 3. The second part of the sentence seems to me to raise a lot of questions. On one level it refers to the content of the speech when Pericles is made to itemize the outstanding qualities of the Athenian *polis* (in a funeral speech, as at a modern memorial service, we expect mention of those qualities associated with the dead which are valued). On another level it hints at the way in which the speech has sometimes been taken as an objective account of historical fact. 'What made Athens great' seems only a hair's breadth away from the inanities of 'the glory that was Greece'.

In this section, therefore, I want to try to dig behind the facade which succeeding generations have erected between us and this speech, and to approach it by asking three plain and simple questions:

1   *Is* it concerned with claims about 'what made Athens great'? (In other words, what does it say? What is it about? What kind of claims are made?)

2   If there is a unified viewpoint in the speech, whose is it? (The historical Pericles' viewpoint? Thucydides'? the mourners'?)

3   What are we to make of it? (Are we in a position to judge whether the viewpoint(s) represented is/are *accurate*, or does it make the kind of claim which is not, in that sense, able to be proved true or false?)

5.1 Subject-matter and context

In order to decide what the speech is about, we need to examine context as well as content. Therefore, please start by reading Thucydides 2.34–46 in your Penguin translation. 2.34 makes the *immediate* context clear, but later we will need to look more broadly at 'context' in the sense of Thucydides' placing of the episode in the structure of Book 2. By all means read also the slightly abbreviated, nineteenth-century translation by Crawley included in *WA* pp.56–9.

As you read:

1   Note down the main features of the society described by Pericles.

2   Decide what, if any, is his overall argument.

3   Consider briefly in what ways the tone and content of his speech reflect the occasion.

In the discussion, I shall try to develop further the basic points you are asked to note.

Discussion

The speech proper begins at 2.36. Notice the mention of the indigenous ancestors of the Athenians. However, this seems like a nod to convention, since here it is the men of the immediately preceding generation who are singled out for especial praise as the founders of the Athenian Empire which was achieved through military prowess. (This generation would presumably be the fathers of the present casualties.) Pericles is not made to regurgitate the 'men of Marathon' theme, but the reference shows it is an accepted part of the framework of values.

Pericles then claims that his speech will be concerned with the Athenian ethos and especially the constitution and way of life. He deals with aspects of this in sequence:

a) *The democracy* (37), which he defines as giving power to the 'whole people', and including equality before the law and acceptance of ability – not wealth – as the criterion for public service. Notice that, in emphasizing *ability*, he avoids getting entangled in the 'mob rule' definition of democracy which we find in the anti-democratic writers. Again, the supposed uniqueness of Athens is stressed. Notice also the reference to 'unwritten laws'. We are not told what these are, but the implication seems to be that there are some values which underpin the sense of communal identity, without being reflected in legislation and political institutions.

b) *Recreation* (38). Note that the term is used in its strict sense to cover games, festivals, domestic ease and security of supply of goods, including 'foreign' luxuries. The theme is taken up in 40–41 where Pericles denies that prosperity leads to 'softness'.

c) *Education* (39 and 41). Note the emphasis on the contrast with Sparta and on the centrality of Athens to the Greek world (a facet of her 'openness').

38–41 are often cited as a celebration of an aesthetic and intellectual ideal. I think such an interpretation is misguided. In fact, the Athenian advantages cited by Pericles are specifically said to be the results of the prosperity resulting from Athenian exploitation of the Empire, which was created and is maintained by military and political qualities. These are set out in the second part of 39. Note the stress on fighting on foreign soil, and note also 41, 'for our adventurous spirit has forced an entry into every sea and every land'. This is an aggressive celebration of war and empire, not a defensive justification. What Pericles is made to do, rather skilfully, is to describe the civic and communal fruits of the underlying military values ('the power which our city possesses and which has been won by these very qualities which I have mentioned'), and then, by turning the argument in a circle, say that this civic prosperity is what makes the city worth fighting and dying for.

There is, too, another reason for Pericles' apparent concentration on the way of life achieved in Athens. This is made clear by the opening and closing sequences (2.35 and 45). By praising the dead mainly through praise of the city, he gives a unity to values, which if applied to individuals would be seen as competitive and hence potentially divisive. Notice especially the repeated recognition of the prevalence of envy and jealousy. Thus what seems, initially, like a piece of anti-rhetorical rhetoric (the deaths of the fallen should be their own memorial, 35) is actually an important pillar of Pericles' overall argument that competition should be directed against those outside Athens and not against fellow citizens. In arguing that courage → freedom → happiness and prosperity (43), he can unite competitive military values and communal civic ones and conclude 'let there be no relaxation in face of the perils of the war'. Thucydides makes Pericles concentrate on eulogy rather than lament. This recognizes the vested interests of the bereaved and thus encourages them to justify past achievements (and maintain the Empire!) *and* look to their own future in competing with the dead (by pursuing the war). ◆

Please now read WA *Chapter 3, 'Human obligations, values and concerns', from 3.1 to 3.14.*

Comment

Notice especially that, in the Funeral Speech, Pericles uses the military competitive values – explored in Homer – as an index of the success of the Athenians abroad, but that within Athenian society he stresses the need to avoid envy, to tolerate others etc. However, *WA* Chapter 3 indicates important respects in which the competitive ethos still dominated social relations *within* Athens as well as *between* Athens and other *poleis*. Later in the block, therefore, we shall look at issues relevant to some of the claims about social relations and values made in the Funeral Speech in order to see whether the claims made there can be substantiated. At this point notice how the values discussed in *WA* relate to one another (helping friends, harming enemies) and how they suggest the existence of competition not only between individuals but between groups. ◆

5.2 Viewpoint

The claim in the funeral speech seems to be that Athenian success in creating and holding an empire before the Peloponnesian War was founded on the competitive values associated with military excellence, and that the best way to maintain the civic advantages gained in the past was to pursue the war (as a *polis*). If we accept this as a coherent viewpoint, then we need to ask 'whose viewpoint?' A number of issues are relevant to this question.

1   First, the speech is supposed to represent a funeral oration. It would then be reasonable to assume that the basic sentiments expressed would not run violently contrary to accepted ideas. Note that it was not only the bereaved who were present but 'everyone who wishes' (citizens *and* foreigners). The occasion might lend itself to a certain propagandist or persuasive element in which the speaker builds onto a shared framework of reference in order to induce the hearers to adopt certain attitudes.

Note also that the Athenians had an important tradition in funeral orations (*epitaphioi*). Demosthenes wrote that 'they alone in the world deliver funeral orations for citizens who have died for their country' (*Against Leptines* 141) – another variant on the 'uniqueness of Athens' theme. Therefore, it is logical to expect a celebration of the city rather than just a lament. It is this convention to which Pericles refers in 2.37. It is Pericles' *choice of aspects* for praise which locates its 'target audience' in place and time and which makes it more than just a general statement of patriotism. (We might compare the oration attributed to Lysias at the beginning of the fourth century, which concentrates on the precedents set up by ancestors and has every sign of being a rhetorical exercise.) This raises a further question to which we can turn later – to whom exactly were the persuasive elements in the speech directed?

2   Then we have to consider the relationship between Thucydides' own views and those of the men to whom he attributes speeches. You should have recalled from Block 3 that it is not possible to accept the speeches simply as verbatim reports. In assessing the Funeral Speech, the question of the author's hindsight also comes in. Was Thucydides attributing to Pericles what Thucydides thought was 'demanded by the occasion' at *that* time (the first year of the war), *or* was he attributing to him what he, Thucydides, thought *with the advantage of hindsight* the occasion demanded, *or* is Thucydides using the speech to set out his own ideas about 'what made Athens great' *or* about what the Athenians thought made them great? And can we realistically distinguish between these four possibilities? Later on I am going to suggest two contrasting readings of the speech, and it will be up to you to decide which (if either) you find convincing, and whether

the two approaches are contradictory or complementary. However, first note two points relevant to the question of whether we are dealing with the viewpoint of Pericles or Thucydides, or a mixture of both:

a) Date of composition

There has been some disagreement between historians about the date of *composition* of the speech. Those who argue for a late date, after 404, tend to regard it as an epitaph for the fall of Athens rather than for the dead of 431. Those who argue for an earlier date of composition point to the way in which Pericles is made to appeal to the achievements of the mid-fifth century and to draw on the communication of confidence associated with a state entering a war. I do not think it is possible to resolve these arguments and some discussions of the problem are anachronistic. (Gomme seems to be imparting early twentieth-century perspectives when he writes that 'he [Pericles] says nothing of the sense of duty, of responsibility, which imperialism should give rise to': *HCT*, vol.2, p.126.) What seems to be *much* more important is where Thucydides locates the speech and the way he relates it to other issues concerned with the Athenian experiences during the first year of the war and immediately following it. Whenever Thucydides composed the speech, it has more than the limited application of a verbatim report. The key to interpretation lies, as so often, in the broader structure of the work.

b) Context and structure of Book 2

Please therefore look again at Thucydides 2.16.2 (Penguin edition p.135), 2.17, 2.19–22, 2.31–2.

Discussion

Notice that the first year of the war had seen both success and set-backs for the Athenians. Their territory had been invaded, the Spartans advancing to within seven miles of Athens (2.21), and there is evidence of disagreement about policy. Pericles' policy was basically defensive (2.22; compare the report, which *is* a late composition, of his last speech, 2.65). Those who had had their land devastated by the invading Spartans were influential (compare Aristophanes' portrayal of the Acharnians, Cassette 3, Band 1), and even if Pericles' policy initially prevailed we know that he used the rhetoric of aggressive imperialism eventually, in order to ensure the support of the Assembly against the land-lobby (see 2.63). Thus we have to interpret the values promoted in the Funeral Speech against the back-drop of policy dispute given to us by Thucydides. Cassette 2, Band 2 discusses evidence about the policy and status of Pericles and gives more suggestions on this subject. If Pericles was faced with more opposition to his policy than Thucydides reveals, then there was special pressure on him to persuade people that the war was being fought to uphold important principles.

The second important point about Thucydides' location of the speech is that it immediately precedes his account of the plague. In 431 Athens was 'at the height of her power and had not yet suffered from the plague' (2.31). The Funeral Oration occupies the pivotal point in the move from high confidence to misery. It is precisely those civic values celebrated in the Funeral Speech which are immediately casualties of the plague. Look especially at the discussion of burial (2.52), and observation of human and unwritten laws (2.53). Thus the structure of Book 2 immediately invites us to recognize *both* the fragility of the value system which Pericles celebrated *and* the relationship of this value system to the rhetoric of political conflict. ◆

5.3 What are we to make of it?

We can now turn to the third of the main questions with which we started, *what are we to make of the Funeral Speech?* I want to approach this from two divergent directions – first, by concentrating on interpretation of the role of this speech in Thucydides, and secondly (and more literally), by using the speech in opening up a series of questions which we will be addressing in the rest of the block.

5.3.1 Interpretation

I am going to summarize two somewhat different interpretations of the significance of this speech and then ask you to keep the implications of each in mind as you work through the rest of the block. We will return to this theme in the Revision Block (Block 6), and you will be asked to assess the validity of these interpretations in the light of your subsequent work. I ought to stress at this point, however, that we are not thinking in terms of judging these (or any other) interpretations as 'right' or 'wrong'. In fact, it may well be useful to consider the extent to which they are, in fact, compatible.

The first interpretation considers the Funeral Speech in Thucydides within the broad tradition of Athenian funeral orations, and categorizes the expressions of values contained in it as an 'invention'. This term is derived from the French title of Nicole Loraux's influential book *The Invention of Athens: The Funeral Oration in the Classical City*, tr. Alan Sheridan (Harvard, 1986). It does not simply mean 'made up' in the sense of telling a story or a lie. It implies rather a self-image, an idealized wish-fulfilling view of the Athenian *polis*, in which the aspirations of the community of the living express themselves through the orator, and the dead are glorified by their association with this civic ideal. In her book, Loraux provides an important example of detailed analysis of the speech from this perspective; and she investigates the form and content of the funeral oration as a genre, including the example found in Thucydides. She finds some evidence of a move in the fifth century towards a more abstract notion of the *polis* (in Aeschylus and Herodotus the city is spoken of in terms of its *citizens*, e.g. Herodotus 7.161 and 9.27; by the time of Thucydides the emphasis is on its *power*, e.g. 1.73.1). Following from this, she argues that in a sense the notion of the *polis* comes between the citizens and the 'real' city, and in this sense the values expressed are an 'invention' – *Athenian history as constructed by the Athenians.*

On this interpretation, it is inappropriate to assess the *epitaphios* as a description of *reality*. Its significance lies in its role as a *model* of how the Athenians saw themselves, of how they would like to have been. Loraux cites Plato's response as evidence of the power of such *epitaphioi*: Plato regarded them as dangerous and illusory because of the gap between the persuasive force of the words (*logoi*) and the objective facts of the city's existence (*erga*). (For a satirical treatment of this, see the extract from *Menexenus ST* 23(c).) (Note that 'invention' as a technical term is not the same as 'ideology'. The word ideology tends to be quite loosely used, but strictly speaking it implies a system of values promoted by one section of a society to persuade other sections to accept domination. Historians have disagreed about whether 'dominant ideology' is a relevant concept for ancient societies. In contrast, 'invention' implies a *communal* self-image.)

A particularly valuable aspect of Loraux's approach is that she starts by identifying the characteristics of the *epitaphios* as an artistic genre in its own right and then considers the significance of the way it is used and adapted in different examples. We might compare the way in which we have studied public buildings and tragic drama in terms of the relationship between the artistic demands of the genre and its status as a social institution. Loraux's thesis built substantially on the work of J.E. Ziolkowski, who produced a detailed analysis of the formal structure of the funeral speech in Thucydides and compared it with other examples of the genre (*Thucydides and the Tradition of Funeral Speeches at Athens*, Arno Press, 1981). Ziolkowski recognized that we lacked the evidence to come to a conclusion about whether the speech was actually delivered by Pericles and, if so, whether he did so in terms comparable to those attributed to him by Thucydides.

However, he argued that it is possible to come to conclusions about the function of this speech in Thucydides' history by setting it in its context in the work *and* by studying the respects in which the structure of the speech approximates to and differs from other surviving examples. In comparing it with other examples of the genre, Ziolkowski stressed that the speech in Thucydides contains much less material on remote ancestors or semi-mythical genealogy than was customary (Thucydides 2.36). The focus is on the empire-founding fathers of the present generation. It is on this point that Loraux bases her contention that the speech is creating a 'civic mythology', grafting current concerns onto the traditional ancestral mythological/historical justification of the uniqueness of Athens. However, it is possible (as my next paragraph tries to describe) to accept the importance of the formal analysis and comparison done by Ziolkowski without being committed to the concept of 'invention' put forward by Loraux.

An alternative interpretation of the role of the speech emphasizes its place in the structure of Thucydides' history. Loraux claims (p.289) that the Funeral Speech was the only speech in Thucydides not necessary to the unfolding of his narrative. This may be true in the sense that it does not refer to 'a moment of decision', but it could be argued that the speech is itself *part* of the narrative *and* explains key stages in it, notably in Pericles' career and in the overarching theme of the decline of Athens. One could also cite the fact that the speech skates over traditional features of the genre (praise of remote ancestors etc.) and concentrates on the present (2.36) as evidence of an immediate political relevance for the ideas expressed.

Such an interpretation would emphasize the immediate rhetorical effect on the Athenians and foreigners present of Pericles' attempt to express a value system which praised open democracy, emphasized the prosperity brought by empire, and promoted co-operation at home and supremacy abroad. From this perspective the speech is shown to be historically rooted in the political crisis arising from conflict in policy about the conduct of the war. Thucydides questions the reality and permanence of the values expressed by placing it next to an episode demonstrating their vulnerability. Other sources could be cited to indicate that, whatever the date of composition, the ideas expressed were familiar in Athenian literature and oratory (for example, Euripides, *The Suppliant Women* 5–15, and the Chorus' speech on the freedom and prosperity of Athens in *Medea* 827ff.).

Such an assessment of Thucydides' *epitaphios* in its historical context turns our attention to the relation between rhetoric and policy in Pericles' career, and to problems about conflict and stability in Athenian society and values as the *polis* faced the impact of war. Under this interpretation, the question of whether there was a *factual* basis for the claims made in the speech is an important one. (Look again at Thucycides 2.41, 'We do not need ... our enemies'.)

5.3.2 Themes and questions

Please now re-read Thucydides 2.35–46, noting down any open or implied claims which seem to you to require investigation or explanation.

Discussion

My list includes just some of the issues which seem to be opened up by the claims made in the Funeral Speech in Thucydides. Keep them in mind as you work through the rest of Block 4. The responses you make to them may help you decide how the speech itself can best be interpreted. (Some of these questions are also taken up in the Revision Block, Block 6.)

1 Was the democracy as 'open' as was claimed? For example, was there really open access to office-holding? Was wealth really unimportant? Did some citizens opt out (the *apragmones*; 2.40)? If so, why? Were they really considered useless? Were there internal disputes about imperial policy or was it more a matter of competition about who should lead the Athenians?

2 How were disputes about policy dealt with? How were decisions really made? Were there checks and balances against the internal effects of envy? Did politically ambitious men operate in groups or individually?

3 Attica covered a wide area. Was only the Assembly important, or did local politics count? Were there pressure groups? How were the interests of town and country reconciled?

4 Was the *polis* really the focus of loyalty? What of individual ambition (*philotimia*) and family reputation? Did the Athenians hang together or did inter-*polis* loyalties and alliances persist?

5 If Athens was a centre of trade and prosperity as the result of empire, who benefited?

6 The Funeral Speech refers only to male citizens (apart from a brief mention of the widows of citizens). Did other social groups contribute to prosperity? If so, why is their role not mentioned? Was Athens as open to foreigners as the speech claims?

7 What were the 'unwritten laws'? Were they kept by everyone? Did all sections of the citizen population really share the same values? ◆

 Two of the articles included in The Offprints are relevant to your study of the Funeral speech (those by Hardwick and by Walcot). It would be useful to read them now. Alternatively, you can study them after you have worked through Section 6.4 of this block, since they both address issues concerning the role of women in Athenian society.

Further Reading

BRUNT, P.A. (1993) 'Thucydides' Funeral Speech', pp.159–80, postscript to Chapter 6, 'Introduction to Thucydides' in *Studies in Greek History and Thought*, Clarendon Press.

HOBSBAWM, E. and RANGER, T. (eds) (1983) *The Invention of Tradition*, Cambridge University Press.

MORRIS, I. (1992) *Death Ritual and Social Structure in Classical Antiquity*, Cambridge University Press ('Key Themes in Ancient History' series).

LORAUX, N. (1986) *The Invention of Athens: the funeral oration in the classical city*, tr. A. Sheridan, Harvard University Press.

ZIOLKOWSKI, J.E. (1981) *Thucydides and the Tradition of Funeral Speeches at Athens*, Arno Press.

6 CITIZENS, POLITICIANS AND THE REST

Study guide

To work on this section you will need *WA*, your Supplementary Texts, your Thucydides set text and The Offprints. We shall be looking at evidence relevant to the themes and questions set out at the end of Section 5. At the end of Section 6 you will be asked to pause and update your notes on those themes. Alternatively you may prefer to do this as you go along.

6.1   The good citizen – *agathos polites*

> We do not say that a man who takes no interest in politics is a man who minds his own business; we say that he has no business here at all.
>
> (Pericles in Thucydides 2.40)

The purpose of this section is to try to investigate precisely what is implied by 'taking an interest in politics' and to try to decide whether there were differences in quality, amount or type of activity undertaken by the ordinary citizen and the more prominent. Remember that, in contrast to the Greeks, we tend to define the sphere of politics in rather a narrow way. But for the Greeks, politics covered 'the affairs of the *polis*', in other words a broad range of activities undertaken in the whole community. A subsidiary aim will be to suggest ways in which the legal and social positions of non-citizen status groups reflect the primacy of the values associated with citizenship.

There is a broad discussion of themes relevant to these issues in WA *Chapters 3 and 5. I suggest you read Chapter 3 now, if you have not already done so. Chapter 5 (omitting the fourth-century material) will be very useful as a revision aid, but you could usefully glance through it now to get some idea of the ground it covers. There is also relevant material in* WA *Chapter 4; I will indicate this as we go along.*

In the rest of this section, I shall try to help you to integrate your reading of *WA* with what you already know, and to suggest some further points and references. To make the integration clearer I shall use four topics to focus the material. Of course, this is not the only possible way to approach the subject and you may want to try out other methods in your tutorial or self-help group.

Topic 1: In the direct democracy what role was there for the ordinary citizens? To what extent was this compulsory/voluntary/prestigious?

The main points are obvious and should be well known to you now. Citizens (males over 18) were liable for military service (for which an allowance was paid) according to their socio-economic class. The better off were liable for the *eisphora*, a property tax used for war finance (see Thucydides 3.19). Citizens could attend the meetings of the Assembly in Athens and address it if they wished. They could attend and vote at ostracisms (held in the Agora).

Assembly attendance was voluntary and (at least for the more boring meetings) had sometimes to be encouraged by 'whipping in' by the slave police who encouraged those in the Agora to go to the Pnyx by using a red-dyed rope (Aristophanes, *Acharnians* 22). From about 400, pay for attendance was introduced. Aristophanes (*Ecclesiazusai*, 183–8, 380–93) indicates that only those who arrived early got their three obols. This indicates that perhaps the main object was to obtain a quorum.

From the age of 30, citizens were eligible for appointment by lot to the various official posts and to the *boule* (on which no-one could serve more than twice). It is not known when pay for serving on the *boule* was introduced, nor is the date for introduction of the lot certain. The lot may have been introduced as part of the reforms of Ephialtes. Prosopography (the study of the careers of individuals) suggests that members of the *boule* tended to come from the higher social classes, even in the second half of the century.

The important exceptions to the operation of the lot are the top military posts, especially the *strategoi* and the *Hellenotamiai* (imperial treasurers) who were elected and could be re-elected. Note that pay for most public offices was withdrawn in 411 under the Five Thousand and abolished by the Four Hundred (?Aristotle, *Constitution of Athens* 33, *ST* 6). This is indirect evidence in support of the view that pay made public office a viable proposition for citizens from a wider range of economic backgrounds. The more oligarchic regimes would want to restrict such participation.

The other important role open to citizens was on the jury-courts. Pericles introduced pay for these after about 462–1, and this was raised in 425 to maintain an equivalence of about half the daily wage of a craftsman. Aristophanes in his play *Wasps* satirizes the eagerness of elderly Athenians to serve on juries (for example, 87–112). Perhaps the pay provided a useful 'pension' or subsistence allowance, but it was not a living wage. The Aristotelian *Constitution of Athens* (*ST* 6, 27) claims that the institution of pay increased the participation of ordinary citizens in the drawing of the lot for jury duty.

The question of compulsory or voluntary participation is a somewhat vexed one. We need to try to distinguish between what was legally enforceable, what was 'expected' and what was undertaken only by a minority but perhaps attracted greater prestige. Military service was expected, and cowardice or desertion were punishable by *atimia* (loss of civic rights; see especially *WA* 5.65–7). The propertied classes had to serve, largely at their own expense. Service in the fleet for *thetes* was initially voluntary, but the pay made it a more attractive proposition (see Old Oligarch 1.13, *ST* 28). (Shortage of manpower is indicated by the enlistment of foreigners and slaves as rowers.)

At the other extreme, to stand for the position of *strategos* involved positive choice and possibly considerable campaigning to ensure election. Offices allocated by lot might involve conscription if candidates were lacking, but the repeated appearances of some individuals in the lists of office-holders suggests the lists were not completed at random. Eligibility for sortition had to be established by checking of citizenship credentials. Some would be more eager to put themselves forward than others, and some rich men took pride in exceeding the minimum contributions (see Lysias 21,1–5, *WA* 5.71). There is some possibility of collusion. All the above refer to participation in the political activities at Athens. *Deme* participation will be considered below.

Topic 2 What criteria were used to define what was 'approved' civic conduct? How was approval expressed?

This is less straightforward than it seems. *WA* Chapter 3 shows clearly the way in which the terms of commendation used in the fifth century were derived from heroic models. Clearly individual combat was no longer appropriate in an age of fleets and hoplites, but success and reputation were still the key ideas, attuned to the requirements of imperialism and democracy. The prestige attached to wealth and social position is shown in evidence from persuasive appeals by speakers in the Assembly and law courts (for example, Alcibiades in the Sicilian debate, Thucydides 6.16, and the rich liturgist exercise in Antiphon *ST* 3(a)), but these are arguments from prominent people in favour of keeping and using their privileges. Such qualities could hardly be required from the ordinary citizen. However, it is clear that wealth and social position were claimed to be a good thing in so far as they were used in services to the State, thus implicitly mitigating the envy of the less well-endowed. (For evidence concerning the sources and use of wealth, see Section 4 of this block.)

Note that the speech prepared for the rich liturgist also indicates that *piety* and *respect for law* are required. In a different sphere, Plato makes Meno, a character in one of his dialogues, put the conventional view (for Socrates to knock down!). Meno is not a poor man but is used as a Platonic dramatic device to put an apparently uncontentious view. In response to a request from Socrates to define *arete* (excellence), Meno replies:

> It's quite easy to explain, Socrates. In the first place, take the *arete* of a man. It's easy to see that the *arete* of a man is to be capable of sharing in political life in such a way as to benefit his friends and damage his enemies while taking care to avoid harm to himself.
>
> (*Meno* 71e, tr. W.K.G. Guthrie, Penguin, 1956)

The one thing that the forensic sources, Meno's view and the ideas expressed in the Funeral Speech have in common is that it is *participation* which is vital. Aristotle claimed: 'The citizen in this strict sense is best defined by the one criterion, "a man who shares in the administration of justice and in the holding of office"' (*Politics* 1275a). I shall take up below the further questions about exactly what 'participation' might entail.

Topic 3: What benefits did the good citizen gain?

Benefits might be both material and intangible. Greek citizenship generally was exclusive, and only citizens could own land in Attica. Athenian citizens participating in state institutions and offices could draw pay when applicable (see above). This provoked criticism in the anti-democratic writers. There were from time to time other benefits, such as the maintenance of war orphans mentioned by Pericles. An inscription dated 403–2 or soon after indicates that this was a political benefit which could be extended to civil war orphans:

> The children of those Athenians who met a violent death during the oligarchy helping the democracy, are because of their fathers' courageous service to the Athenian democracy, to have maintenance of an obol a day.
>
> (Hesperia 40,1971, including discussion by R.S. Stroud, pp.280–301)

Citizenship also entailed eligibility for material benefits such as the rare grain distribution (from Egypt, 445).

The main intangible benefit is described by the Greek word *time*, meaning reputation or honour. We need not assume that desire for public approval was confined to the few most prominent citizens. A glance at our own society will show that there may be honour and respect attached to quite local prominence – large splashes in small puddles. Unfortunately the written sources, concerned as they are with the great and famous, tell us all too little about the smaller fry.

Topic 4: Is there a uniform pattern of activity for the ordinary and the prominent? Are there imbalances in the sources available to us?

The questions of uniformity of activity and criteria of judgement across the whole citizen body are complicated. However, a check on the main sources we have so far encountered alerts us to some problems. Sources such as Thucydides, Xenophon, and the Aristotelian *Constitution of Athens* are concerned with the role of prominent politicians, the tensions between individuals and groups contending for power, and with the pattern of constitutional development. Their interests are essentially urban, concentrating on decisions and influences at Athens.

The Old Oligarch's commentary on the relationship between participatory offices (generally uniting sortition and pay) and elected offices (election supposedly on the basis of expertise and reputation) was a typically anti-democratic polarization between the many and the 'respectable' few (see *ST* 28).

But when we look, for example, at the plays of Aristophanes we become aware that there are citizens 'in between' who fall into neither of the extreme categories. Just occasionally such people surface in other sources, although not by name.

Look at Thucydides 2.20–1.

Here the land of the Acharnians, an important and prosperous *deme* only seven miles from Athens (see Course Guide Map 5) is invaded by Sparta, and the Acharnians put pressure on the Athenians as a whole to march out in their support. We need not concern ourselves here with the relation between Archidamus' provocative action and Pericles' defensive policy (I will take this up later). The important point is that we have a brief insight into the concerns and influence of a prosperous rural community. (However, the figure of 3,000 hoplites is debatable.) The Acharnians are in one sense a 'special case', as their treatment in both Aristophanes and Thucydides shows. But Thucydides' brief and unusual mention of the Acharnians indicates to us that there are elements of Athenian political life at local and *deme* level which are important and on which the major written sources are largely silent. We need to try to find out how these communities related to life and decision-making in the city, how they organized themselves. Were they merely 'feeders' to the operation of the democracy in the city (by organizing the lot), or did they themselves operate a microcosm of the democratic organization with its attendant values?

Unfortunately we do not have the evidence to answer these questions with any certainty and particularly not for the fifth century. However, there is important epigraphic evidence relating to the fourth century, reinforced to an extent by material from forensic oratory. The evidence is collected and discussed in D.Whitehead, *The Demes of Attica, 508/7–c.250 BC* (Princeton, 1986), which also includes appendices of *deme* documents and a prosopography.

The *deme* system itself reflects a compromise between democratic organization and the traditional emphasis on kinship. Kleisthenes' reforms (see *WA* H.I.11) changed the basis of political organization from kinship to location, but *deme* membership was also hereditary, so by the time with which we are concerned membership is a question of kinship as much as residence, although doubtless the two often coincided.

We know that in the fifth century the *deme* officials had responsibility for the organization of some aspects of the democratic process – the initial *dokimasia* (examination of officials before they took office, see *WA* glossary), the lot, etc. Scholars disagree about the extent to which procedures for registration and admission to the *deme* were standardized in the early fifth century, but certainly the age or status of the candidate were examined (citizen status of the mother as well as the father was required after Pericles' citizenship law of 451–0).

It is likely that regular *deme* assemblies were held (perhaps in Athens during the evacuation) and that demes were responsible for the organization and upkeep of local cults. (A decree dated 450–440 records the cult finances of Nemesis at Rhamnous 1G 1³248.) There is, also, some evidence of the organization of festivals, perhaps in conjunction with the rural Dionysia. For example, an inscription recording an Ikarian decree (1G 1³254) indicates that dramatic festivals took place in honour of Dionysos. (Fourth-century evidence confirms that *deme* liturgies later became well established, and that *philotimia*, literally love for one's reputation, was given a communal focus in honorific inscriptions.)

We also have fifth-century evidence to indicate a sense of solidarity among fellow *deme*smen. It is true that identification by *deme* rather than by use of the father's name (son of X) was not generally established. (Those from prominent families tended to use the latter, and Thucydides, for example, never uses the demotic when mentioning individuals.) Nevertheless, there seems to be some overlap between the notions of *philoi* (friends) and *demotai* (*deme*smen). For example, in *Clouds* 1218–9 there is a reference to unwillingness to be the enemy of a fellow *deme*sman (and see also 1206–10), while in Lysias 27.12 (early fourth century) a defendant's *demotai* and *philoi* join together in begging for mercy. This suggests *deme* relationships could be a positive force. However, this was by no means sufficient to ensure overall unity in the *polis*. Contrast Thucydides 8.66, where the historian suggests that fear in the city in 411 was increased because the citizens did not know each other well enough to know whom could be trusted.

Figure 27 Extract from the financial regulations of the Deme Skambonidai at Athens *c.*460. The inscription includes part of the oath taken at the beginning of the term of office and refers to the financial examination undertaken at the end. The restored text reads: '...as it may] be heralded (and) announced. I shall both safeguard the common (property) of the Skambonidai and I shall return to the Public Examiner what is due. These things (they are) to swear (by) the three gods. Whatever of the common (property) they do not give back to the Public Examiner...' (Cat.GR1785.5–27.2, British Museum, IG 1³244).

So far the balance of the evidence I have mentioned suggests a degree of congruence between the political organization and political values in the city and in the *demes*. However, a further question remains: were the same people prominent in both, was *deme* prominence a step towards prominence in the *polis* as a whole, or were the two areas relatively separate? Again, the evidence is far from complete. Common sense tells us that *deme* participation gave useful administrative experience, but the use of the lot meant that even the most willing could not be sure of the opportunity to serve at the chosen time either in *deme* or *polis*. Simon Hornblower has pointed out (*The Greek World 479–323 BC*, p.118) that there is a suspicious tendency for *prominent* politicians to appear in the right office at the right time; for example, Kleon was a member of the council in 427, fathers and sons served at the same time. Perhaps the lot could be manipulated, but surely this was more likely to be in favour of the already prominent? The merely aspiring would lack the necessary *time* (reputation), unless bribery was used. It seems unlikely for other reasons that progression through *deme* offices would be desirable as a means to power. The evidence from prosopography suggests that different individuals were prominent in the *demes* and the *polis*, perhaps because it was clearly necessary to be at Athens in order to attend the Assembly and achieve influence and elected office. (See Section 6.4 below for the essentially urban commitment of the political orators, the *rhetores*.) The skills required to succeed in the Assembly at Athens could hardly be acquired in the *demes* – the opportunities to propose a *deme* decree must have been relatively limited.

A final possibility remains – that *deme* solidarity could be used as a power base for those aspiring to elected office in the *polis*. Some sources refer to Kimon's distribution of largesse to his *deme*smen (for example, Plutarch, *Kimon.* 10 and ?Aristotle, *Constitution of Athens* 27, ST 6). In this context Plutarch's evidence is probably governed by Roman models and should not carry much weight. The *Constitution of Athens* is interesting for the claim that after the democratic changes of the 460s, wealth became less decisive as a determinant of power when other methods of achieving and holding power were required by the democracy. However, it still seems to have been a *necessary* condition, if no longer a *sufficient* condition.

Certainly, if the *deme* had significance as a power base, we would expect it to be used by, for example, Nikias and Alcibiades, both conspicuously wealthy men. Yet there is no reference in our main sources to exploitation of *deme* ties by these men. Perhaps such exploitation grew progressively more difficult during the fifth century as ties of residence lessened among *deme*smen and alternative means of political dominance grew more important.

On balance, therefore, I think we can conclude that, on one level, *deme* participation was an important aspect of being a good citizen and, in the fifth century, represents a range of scantily documented political activity, an essential part of 'taking an interest in politics'. However, it did not provide an important focus or springboard for the small number of politically ambitious men. We shall turn in Section 6.5 to consideration of the framework within which *they* operated. However, first we need to consider briefly what were the attitudes to the citizens who did not fit in with the conventional criteria, and to the non-citizens.

6.2 The *apragmones* and the *polypragmones*

In Book 2.40 Thucydides makes Pericles refer explicitly to those who did not participate. He says this is not just a question of minding one's own business (being *apragmon*) but of being useless (*achreios*). Your set text translates this as 'having no business here at all', but the word has associations with sickness, old age and physical weakness. The inference, therefore, is that those who do not participate are passengers in the community. Previously, Pericles has claimed (2.37.1) that no one is kept in obscurity by poverty, and it seems reasonable to allow that the institution of state pay did in general permit participation of the ordinary citizen in the democratic processes outlined in the previous section. However, in 2.40 Pericles' attention is not directed at those who did not participate on grounds of poverty. The association he makes is particularly between being inactive (*apragmon*) and useless. He thus appears to be commenting on the dichotomy between inactivity and activity as political stances.

The opposite to *apragmon* is, strictly speaking, *polypragmon*, which had associations not just of political activity, but perhaps of *over*-activity or meddling. It was sometimes used as a term of abuse against democratic leaders and imperialists like Kleon. When Thucydides wanted to present a positive image of the 'vigorous' or 'energetic' Spartan general Brasidas, whom he admired, he resorted to a rare word – *drasterios* (4.81).

Once we establish that the nouns *apragmosune* and *polypragmosune* and their derivatives are used as slogans to describe political individuals, we need to ask what policies or attitudes are implied. (Compare the use of 'wet' and 'dry' as political epithets in the 1980s. The terms imply the holding of different attitudes, but participation in politics is an active ingredient in both.) Consider Thucydides 6.18.6–7 where Nikias is called *apragmon* by Alcibiades. Clearly we cannot say Nikias is a non-participant in politics. The epithet is used to draw attention to disagreement over policy and attitudes.

L.B. Carter has examined a sequence of references to *apragmosune* in Athenian politics (*The Quiet Athenian*, Oxford, 1986 – the title itself involves a pun on *apragmon*), and has usefully focused attention on the multiplicity of reasons why citizens might not wish to be energetically involved in politics. Reasons put forward by Carter include: the unwillingness of the peasant farmer to become urbanized (but note the distinction between participation and prominence in 6.1 above, and in particular the opportunities for participation in *deme* politics); the unwillingness of those who preferred a contemplative or retired life; the unwillingness of rich aristocrats to be involved with the developed democracy; the unwillingness of men who already enjoyed affluence and reputation to hazard themselves and their property in the political arena. (The audit or *euthynai* which followed the year of office was in two parts: the first financial, the second a general review in which any citizen was able to bring an accusation.) Three at least of these four categories of *apragmones* suggest elements of opposition to the dynamic policy of the imperial democracy, and it could therefore be that a political argument underlies Pericles' rejection of them in the Funeral Speech. They might not be so much useless as *dangerous* passengers.

It is, however, important not to see such people as representing a unified opposition or indeed a 'peace party' in the 420s. They represent a disparate range of interests – attachment to their land holdings, desire for an individual political prominence thwarted by the democracy, inter-*polis* aristocratic links, desire to continue to draw on the material advantages of empire now threatened by war, perhaps quasi-philosophical objections to the democracy. It took the compulsory urbanization brought about by the evacuation of Attica, and the economic and political chaos of defeats in the war, to bring these dissident interests to an uneasy accommodation (411 and 404). Not until after the war do we see the philosophical objections to democracy fully articulated in the literary sources.

The *apragmones* were the objects of disapproval in the context of the values expressed in the Funeral Speech. But in other contexts, in other political perspectives, at least some of those covered by the term might be considered admirable. In a more positive way the word *sophrosune* (prudence, soberness, temperance, moderation) becomes what Simon Hornblower has described as 'an oligarchic code word', used to praise a conservative abstinence from the *polypragmosune* of full democracy and empire.

6.3 The non-citizen

The community (*koinonia*) also had two groups with legally and socially defined roles which need brief consideration – *metics* and women. To these we should add foreigners. I will not be saying anything about slaves here, since in Greek terms they belong more clearly to the study of material resources which we looked at in Part 1 of this block (Section 4).

6.3.1 Foreigners

The Funeral Speech speaks of the openness of Athens to foreigners (2.39). In one sense this was true: Athens was an open city and did not practise the periodic deportations characteristic of Sparta. Foreigners are specifically mentioned as being able to be present at the funeral of those killed in the first year of the war and at the departure of the Sicilian Expedition. The corollary is that both displays contain elements of state propaganda designed to impress foreigners.

But there were important and strict limits to the openness of Athens. The term foreigner covers both Greek and non-Greek, although most visitors would probably be Greeks, on official business from other *poleis*, attending festivals, engaged in trade and so on (see WA 4.71, but note that the example quoted of a state decree refers to the late fourth century).

Residence was, however, limited to one month, and after this a foreigner had to register as a *metic* and pay a regular tax. Foreigners had no access to citizen rights and were under special disabilities. The law regarded assault or killing of a foreigner less severely than that of a citizen. Foreigners could be required to give evidence under torture (the fourth-century orators provide examples). The children of foreigners and Athenians were denied citizenship after 451/0. We can see from Old Comedy that the accusation of foreign ancestry became a conventional taunt in political argument. The position of foreigners and the attitudes to them are thus further confirmation of the exclusive status of the citizenship, which existed alongside (and was perhaps intensified by) the cosmopolitan nature of Athenian commercial and imperial activity.

Some foreigners had special political significance; these were the 'guest friends' of the Athenian aristocracy and the *proxenoi* of the Athenians in other *poleis*, and we will look at the implications of these relationships in Section 6.4.

6.3.2 *Metics*

Metics were resident foreigners (see the discussion in WA 4.67–71). They had to register in a *deme* under the patronage of an Athenian citizen and pay a tax of one drachma a month (half of this rate for an independent woman). This was not a particularly onerous amount (the allowance for a serving hoplite was a drachma a day) so many *metics* could have been employed for their craft skills, working alongside both citizens and slaves for the same wage. Note that manumitted slaves became *metics* not citizens.

Analysis of the occupations of *metics* identified from inscriptions suggests that 39.9% were engaged in crafts and industry, 8.5% as industrial entrepreneurs, 20.9% in merchanting and retail trade, 12.4% were women in employment, 9.8% miscellaneous and 8.5% in agriculture (Gerhardt's figures, quoted by Davies, *Wealth*, p.50). These figures have been distorted by the inclusion of manumitted slaves. They also exclude those engaged in the liberal arts (including teachers, sophists etc.). The Old Oligarch refers to the fact that 'the city needs *metics* because of all its industries' (12, ST 28). *Metics* had limited access to public activities (courts, theatres, festivals) but could not own land. The more prosperous were eligible to provide liturgies and were liable for property taxes. They could also serve in the fleet and the army. Thucydides refers to the participation of *metic* hoplites in the invasion of the Megarid (2.31). This may have marked the first occasion on which they served in a campaign outside Attica.

The fact that *metics* were registered in *demes* (although they could not hold office) provides useful evidence about their distribution through Attica. An early piece of evidence, a lex sacra of c.460 (Figure 27) shows the *deme* Skambonidai permitting the *metics* to participate in one of its sacrifices. Unfortunately this inscription is the only one of its kind in existence, so we cannot judge whether it is typical. However, there is significant evidence, dating from the last quarter of the fifth century to the last quarter of the fourth, indicating that of 366 *metics* whose *deme* residence is known, 82% lived in just eight *demes*, concentrated (not surprisingly) in urban and sub-urban Athens, the Piraeus and Eleusis. The remainder were fairly evenly distributed across the remaining *demes* (Whitehead, *Demes*, p.83).

After 451/0 *metics* could not marry citizens and have citizen status for their children, and opportunities for *metics* to attain citizen status directly were few. (The career of the banker Pasion mentioned in WA 4.70 is fun to read but only significant in the sense that it was almost unique.) More interesting is the evidence of the ambivalent attitude to *metics* in the upheavals at the end of the fifth century.

Look up ST 17(b) where you will find a fuller version of the inscription referred to in WA 4.68.

This recorded the grant of citizenship to *metics* who had fought alongside the democrats at Phyle during the regime of the Thirty Tyrants. They were probably encouraged by the promise of citizenship.

At about the same time, the orator Lysias, whose father had been attracted to Athens by Pericles, was offered the citizenship, but the offer was withdrawn after the prosecution of the mover of the decree. Lysias had already had unfortunate experiences under the Thirty, when his wealthy family became the victims of denunciation and confiscation and his brother was killed. After the restoration of the democracy Lysias prosecuted Eratosthenes for the murder, but his speech makes clear that this was alleged to be part of a concerted policy against rich *metics* with confiscation an instrument of economic policy: look up the extract in *ST* 20.

Thus in general, in so far as the fifth-century evidence allows us to study the experiences of *metics* and attitudes towards them, their position seems to reflect the prevailing political climate – relatively stable and prosperous in the 430s, uncertain by the end, but the upheavals at the end of the century reflect political conflict rather than any far-reaching changes in *metic* status. The fourth century saw restoration of internal stability and continuity in the relation between *metic* and citizen status. (For a detailed study, see D. Whitehead, *The Ideology of the Athenian Metic*, 1977.)

6.4 Athenian women

Probably the most overworked quotation on this subject is Pericles: 'the greatest glory of a woman is to be least talked about by men, whether they are praising you or criticizing you' (Thucydides, 2.46). The context and phrasing indicate that the remark was probably addressed to the war-widows. John Purkis has reminded me that 'men tend to say this sort of thing precisely when women are most voluble'. So perhaps we should decode the wish expressed here and, rather than accepting the statement as referring to a norm, we could speculate about what Pericles was reacting against.

Figure 28 Attic red figure kylix, provenance unknown. Interior, woman filling a winecup, by Oltos *c*.510 (diameter 32.75cm., 13in.) (Cat.1927.4065 ARV 62.77).

There is substantial treatment of the position of women in *WA*, and if the topic interests you, I suggest you look this up by using the index. However, the issue does raise some methodological problems which need consideration. Firstly, we are in a position only to study Athenian women through the eyes and attitudes of men. The written sources for the fifth and fourth centuries are entirely male (the poet Sappho had her circle on Lesbos in the sixth century) and were not produced with the aims of giving information about women. They were produced with the aims of settling disputes about citizenship, property and killing (the forensic orators), promoting efficient management of the *oikos* (Xenophon, *Oikonomikos*), and for recording the procedures of religious ritual (inscriptions and literary sources). This is not to deny the importance of women's role in such matters, but the importance is a matter of *function* in maintaining and transmitting the framework of values set and represented by the male citizens. A possible exception in the sources is the portrayal of feeling in some of the white ground vases (see Illustration Booklet II.23 and 50), but even here it is arguable that what is presented is an aspect of the dependence of the (widowed) females as depicted by male artists.

It is because of the nature of the sources that I have decided to include this short section on women as part of a larger section dealing with the practices, values and attitudes associated with citizenship. Athenian women were in the slightly ambivalent situation of being and not being citizens. They were citizens in the sense of being part of the network of citizens, laws and attitudes, and had some rights. They were not citizens in the sense that they did not participate in *polis* or *deme* assemblies or public offices. Nor did they participate in war, other than as victims. It is clear that it was not customary for citizen women to go about or work in public (there was plenty of work within the *oikos*) and that it was part of the good reputation of the citizen to guard jealously the women of the *oikos*.

The term conventionally given to this way of defining women's lives is 'seclusion'. It is important to distinguish between seclusion and contempt. The latter term may seem a plausible label for those viewing through twentieth-century perspectives, but the fact remains that seclusion for an Athenian woman was a concomitant of the importance of the functions she was supposed to fulfil. That said, there is evidence to support the view that her dependent position was the result not only of safeguarding her functions, but perhaps also of fear and revulsion towards the supposed potential of her nature. This broad question is discussed by J.P. Gould in his Offprints article, 'Law, custom and myth: aspects of the social position of women in Classical Athens'. You will find material relevant to a study of women's history in other sections of this course, notably in the discussion of the use of space in domestic architecture (Sections 4.1.5 and 4.1.6 of this block), on religious cults in TV7, and in your study of *The Women of Troy* in Section 8 of this block and of *The Bacchae* in Block 5. You can also use Illustration Booklet II as a source for studying how women and their activities were presented by artists. The illustrations in *WA* Chapters 2 and 4 are also useful and could be approached in conjunction with Colin Cunningham's discussion in Section 3.3 of this block. Here I propose only to identify the main aspects highlighted by our analysis of the values of the Athenian citizen, and to consider whether there is any evidence of tension or questioning of these values during our period.

At this point, please refer to WA *4.23–39 for outline information on the position of women in Athens. (There is further material elsewhere in* WA *which you can locate by using the index if you wish to study the topic in more detail.)*

Note especially that after Pericles' citizenship law of 451/0, the wife had to be a citizen to ensure citizen status for the heirs. If raped or caught in adultery, she therefore had to be divorced. The *epikleros* or heiress was used to transmit property in the absence of male heirs. She had to marry the nearest male relative. As Richard Garner puts it, 'she had no more choice in the matter than would a tripod or a vase' (*Law and Society in Classical Athens*, Croom Helm, 1987, p.84).

Something to be emphasized in the Greek context is that the management of the *oikos* was no trivial pursuit. When Plato's Meno says, 'Take a woman's *arete*. That's easy to define. It's the need to look after the household properly, checking the contents and obeying her husband' (*Meno* 71e), he is not only assuming dependence and seclusion, he is also implying skilled management and hard physical work (if domestic slaves were not kept). In a society lacking domestic technology, matters such as correct storage and preservation of foodstuffs were crucial.

Of course, there were exceptions to the general convention of seclusion. No system of social behaviour can be unaffected by war and defeat, and we have references in fourth-century forensic oratory to possible changes during the emergency before and after the fall of Athens (e.g. Demosthenes, *Against Eubulides* 35, ST 8). There are also the 'unique' exceptions. However, the fact that Aspasia could jokingly be said to have acted as Pericles' speech-writer (see Plato, *Menexenus*, ST 23(c)) or that her name was found recorded on a lead curse tablet (both she and her legal 'helpers' were cursed, 1G 3³106) doesn't permit us to draw conclusions about the influence of women in public life. Aspasia, like Pasion, was not an Athenian and is a unique exception. It is an entertaining speculation as to how far her role was exaggerated by Pericles' enemies in order to embarrass him. Perhaps the subject became a standing joke. So far as the unrecorded and private influence of women on public affairs via their husbands is concerned, we just do not know – either way.

Some of Aristophanes' plays, notably *Lysistrata* and *Ecclesiazusai*, explore the comic possibilities of positive intervention by women in public affairs – in *Lysistrata* an attempt to end hostilities, in *Ecclesiazusai* a takeover of the Assembly. How we interpret these is really governed by our understanding of the relation of comedy generally to its social subject-matter. There is particular mileage in presenting the impossible as actually happening. Perhaps Aristophanes was actually reflecting 'women's gossip'. More likely he was mocking the situation to which a society is brought when the normal hierarchy and order is 'turned upside down'. However, it may be that in *Ecclesiazusai* he was also drawing on current debate about communism, and that this included the idea of the community of women. Aristophanes takes up the corollary, the participation of women in the community.

This whole question of the re-ordering and reconstruction of society is taken up in the early fourth century by Plato in his dialogue *The Republic*, and here there is an important section (450–466, extract in ST 23(b)) in which some women are given an almost equal social and political role (women are to bear a lighter share owing to inferior physical strength).

Read this now.

Three things are significant:

a) This applies only to the class of guardians, or rulers.

b) Although women are said to be physically weaker, they are assumed to be mentally and morally the equal of men (this was a revolutionary idea).

c) The concomitant of the participation of women in public life and war is that for the guardian class the individual *oikos* will be abolished. Community living will be the rule, and breeding of citizens will be from carefully selected couples, the children being reared in state nurseries.

For our purposes, this sequence in Plato is significant for two reasons. Firstly, it shows by implication how strongly the position of women in classical Greece was bound into the framework of citizen values and practices. To tamper with one part means rethinking the whole. Secondly, it shows the extent to which Plato was a revolutionary thinker reacting against the events and traditions of his time. Because of his subsequent influence we tend to think of him as an outstanding example of Greek thought. However, the truth is that his effect in his own time was negligible (like Pasion and Aspasia, his significance is in highlighting deviance from the norm!). The mass of evidence from fourth-century orators pleading cases of citizenship, inheritance and so on suggests that so far as the position of the wives of Athenian citizens was concerned, there was essential continuity in conventional values from the fifth to the fourth century. As the speech writer put it: 'We have *hetairai* for the sake of pleasure, mistresses for the daily refreshment of our bodies, but wives to bear us legitimate children and to look after the home faithfully' (Ps. Demosthenes *Against Neaira* 122).

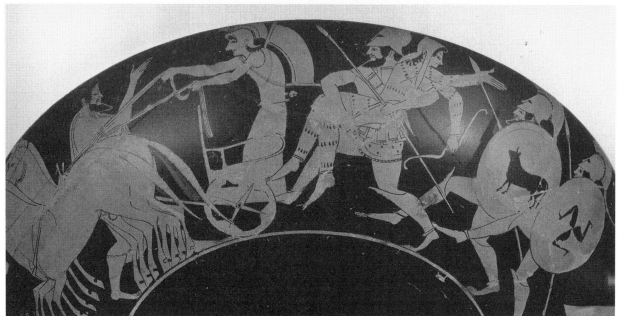

Figure 29 A and B Attic red figure kylix, exterior of Figure 28. Theseus and the rape of Antiope. Theseus was the legendary king of Athens who, after unifying Attica, took part with Heracles in an expedition against the Amazons in which Antiope was abducted. Note the conjunction of the two scenes on this kylix.

To round out your work on this section, turn now to The Offprints and work through the section which introduces and comments on the articles by Walcot, Hardwick and Gould. You will need to allow time to read these three articles with care and to consider the implications of the different perspectives which they bring to the issues surrounding the role of women in Greek society. *It is important to have read thoroughly the introduction to The Offprints before studying individual articles.*

6.5 The politically active citizen

In turning our attention to a special group among the citizens – those who were politically active beyond the requirements of participation, i.e. those who actively sought prominence – we run into some problems of terminology and methodology. In the first place, as we discovered in Section 6.2, the terms *apragmones* and *polypragmones* tend to be slogans implying approval or disapproval of certain political stances rather than merely descriptive terms used to describe degrees of political activity. In identifying the politically active citizen, it therefore seems to make sense to try to identify what he did and the methods used. Secondly, different types of source tend to give a one-sided view. It is particularly hard, for example, to arrive at a balanced treatment of the working of the democratic political system in its different stages. Inscriptions may record what the Assembly decided and what was decreed. They do not tell us how the decision was reached. Lists of office-holders may tell us who was prominent and when, but they do not yield direct evidence about the background to the election of particular *strategoi*, for instance. The written sources such as the Aristotelian *Constitution of Athens*, the Old Oligarch and Thucydides, are hostile to the developed democracy, while late sources such as Plutarch may seriously distort our perceptions by focusing on the biographies of outstanding individuals and attempting to explore what were in fact personal rivalries for power in terms of spurious disagreements about policy.

I am therefore going to make a path through this minefield of conceptual and methodological difficulties by asking three simple sets of questions:

1   How did the politically ambitious Athenian make his way and what did he have to do to succeed?

2   What challenges did he face and how was political defeat brought about?

3   What tensions and changes can we identify during the fifth century?

6.5.1 Making his way

There are three main points to bear in mind. Firstly, the values associated with being a good citizen required commitment across the spectrum of military, civic, social and political participation. Therefore a political career was in one sense rather less specialized than would be the case in our own society, for example. (This is a counterbalance to the stress on political skills which will be mentioned later.) Secondly, the Athenians did not have political parties in the sense that we know them, i.e. bureaucratic organizations acting both as a focus of interests and as a means of advancement with a career structure. This is not to say that groups of Athenians did not act together or form alliances over particular issues, but that there was no structure running parallel to the offices of state. A political career was pursued *in* the institutions of the *polis*. The third point is closely related to this: since so many offices were allocated by sortition, the need for pressure groups to ensure election was limited. Moreover, since the democracy was a *direct* one, the need for pressure groups was to ensure success in votes on key *issues* as they arose, rather than to ensure *election* of groups of people supporting particular policies. Therefore, the ambitious politician had to ensure either that he obtained an important elected office, or that he succeeded in influencing the Assembly and Council at key moments of decision, or both. To do this he had to obtain support both outside and inside the Assembly. These are the main sources of support, with brief comment on their strengths and limitations:

1   Family ties

In Block 1 Section 6, we considered examples of the prominence of some politically active families in the first part of the century. Refer back to Herodotus' treatment of the ensuing rivalries. The development of the full democracy restricted 'dynastic' ambitions. However, even after the institution of the *deme* system, registration in the extended kinship group or *phratry* (see *WA*

Glossary) could still be adduced as evidence of citizenship if an individual was challenged. This shows that ties of kinship were by no means entirely replaced by ties of locality. (The persistence of the patronymic rather than the demotic in written sources was noted earlier.)

A rather different form of kinship group was the *genos* (pl. *gene*), a privilege group claiming descent from a common ancestor, often mythical. The most important ties of obligation were common religious ceremonies of burial places, mutual rights of succession to property and (most important) reciprocal obligations of help, defence and redress of injuries (cf. *philoi* below). The names of 65 Athenian *gene* have been established by historians (P. MacKendrick, *The Athenian Aristocracy 399 to 31 BC*, Martin Classical Lectures Vol.23, Harvard University Press, 1969). Their degree of political influence in the fifth century is disputed, but those who are known to have belonged to *gene* include Themistokles, Aristeides, Kimon, Pericles, Thucydides son of Melesias, Thucydides the historian, Alcibiades.

The account in ?Aristotle *Constitution of Athens* 28 (*ST* 6) suggests that up to the death of Pericles, most of the Athenian leaders – including those whose reforms led to the extension of democracy – came from aristocratic propertied families.

Professor Davies has also shown by prosopographical study that throughout the fifth century, there was considerable overlap between the propertied classes and the highest military offices, to such an extent that over one-third of known hipparchs and *strategoi* can be shown to come from propertied families (*Wealth*, p.122). Both the Old Oligarch (1.3, *ST* 28) and Aristotle (*Politics*, 1282a 31–32) refer to the persistence of this connection in the fifth century. Therefore, we can conclude that birth, wealth and family ties provided both a framework of expectations and training as well as a network of influence.

2 Friendship

The political implications are outlined in *WA* Chapter 3. The obligations of kinship slide into those of friendship, but friendship becomes more important as a basis for political support as the scope for appeal to extended family ties diminishes.

3 Demes

For discussion of the limited evidence on this, see Section 6.1.

4 Clubs

The *hetaireiai* were upper-class dining clubs (they required wealth and leisure). *Philoi* came together socially, but sometimes the club was a basis for political activity. The political clubs were sometimes seen as the bases for factions: for example, the Aristotelian *Constitution of Athens*, discussing the establishment of the rule of the Thirty Tyrants, comments, 'those of the nobles who belonged to the Political clubs ... aimed at an oligarchy' (*ST* 6). The word *hetaireia* itself could be used to suggest conspiracy, and *hetairoi* is used initially as a synonym for conspirators by Thucydides in connection with the murder of Androkles (Book 8.65). Where the Penguin translation has 'party', the Greek often has *hetairoi* or sometimes the more neutral *hoi amphi* or *hoi peri* (those around, i.e. associates).

5 Factions

Sometimes the term is used to describe a clique or group, but it becomes a term of abuse. The Greek word for faction, *stasis*, is the same word used for civil strife (for example, Thucydides 3, 82–3). Plutarch refers (*Pericles* 11.2) to Thucydides son of Melesias packing the assembly with his faction, and the persistence of such tactics is suggested by the requirement imposed in 410 by the restored democracy that members of the Council should swear to take their seats by lot (referred to by Philochorus in a fragment 328 F 140). Thucydides 6.13 has Nikias referring to the intimidating presence of Alcibiades' supporters in the Assembly, although the word for faction is not used.

Notice how the membership and scope of all the above groups (1–5) can slide towards one another. We are clearly here with a *network* of associations and influences. Such networks were not of course confined to Athens and we need to mention ways in which inter-*polis* contacts could be used politically:

6   Inter-polis relations – xenoi and proxenoi

Aristocratic families in the Greek *poleis* traditionally had ties of friendship and hospitality, and this persisted into the fifth century. An interesting example is the relationship between Pericles and the Spartan Archidamus.

Look up Thucydides Book 2.13.

Archidamus was the *xenos* or guest-friend of Pericles, which implies reciprocal obligations of friendship and hospitality. Such ties could bring both personal and diplomatic advantages. However, in time of war such a relationship was a political disadvantage to Pericles, and he took steps to distance himself from adverse criticism.

A formal institution was that of *proxenos*, in which a citizen might be officially appointed to look after the interests of another state in his own *polis*. WA 5.95 gives an example of a proxeny decree by which Athens appointed a citizen of another *polis* as *proxenos* to further her interests there. The role of *proxenos* could be important diplomatically. Prosopographical study also provides an index of the external relationships of leading citizens in Athens, and suggests a further network of influences and intrigue, diplomacy and intelligence-gathering (M. Walbank, *Athenian Proxenies of the Fifth Century*, 1978).

7   Activities

What the ambitious political leader had to *do* was modified somewhat during the century. The initial importance of the office of war-archon gave way to that of *strategos*, and with the reforms of Ephialtes the *ekklesia* and *boule* took political prominence from the Areopagus (WA H.I.27 and ?Aristotle *Constitution of Athens* 25, ST 6).

M.H. Hansen has identified a core of activities, all of which by the fourth century were vital to a rising politician (*The Athenian Assembly*, Blackwell, 1987). These are:

> Proposal of a decree in *boule* or *ekklesia*
> Proposal of a law (*nomos*)
> Delivery of a speech in *boule* or *ekklesia*
> Prosecution or defence in a public political legal action
> Mission as an ambassador
> Administration of public money as an elected treasurer.

We will return to these. At this stage, note that the activities confirm the increasing need to be present in Athens, that particular knowledge and skills are involved and that *most of these activities can be carried out by men who do not at that time necessarily hold any particular elected office*. The absence of a public prosecutor or regular civil service enhanced the importance of these activities in the running of the *polis* and also gave a key role to the *private* prosecution. Although *isegoria* or the right to speak was open to 'anyone who wishes', knowledge was required in order to make an effective contribution. (This point is taken up in the anti-democratic writers: for example, Xenophon *Memorabilia* 3.6, and Plato *Protagoras* 319c.)

6.5.2 Political challenges

Attaining political prominence was competitive and public. Holding it was even more so. We can explore this by looking at the institution and mechanisms of 1) ostracism, 2) the *graphe*, 3) the *euthunai* (rendering of accounts or audit).

As you read on, bear in mind the list of activities of the aspiring politician quoted above and the network of influences outlined in the previous section.

1 Ostracism

The first recorded ostracism was in 487. Sources and opinions differ about whether the law was instituted then or 20 years earlier by Kleisthenes. (It was found in other *poleis* – for example, Argos, Megara, Miletus and in Syracuse.) Each year the question was put to the *ekklesia* as to whether an ostracism should be held. If the vote was in favour, the ostracism took place in the Agora. Each citizen who wanted to participate voted with a potsherd on which was inscribed the name of the citizen whom he wished to be banished (see Figure 30). Providing at least 6,000 votes were cast against him, the candidate with the most votes was ostracized. He had to leave within ten days and stay away for ten years, but did not forfeit citizenship or property and could return when the period expired. Ostracism thus marked political or personal defeat, but not condemnation or disgrace. Among those known to have been ostracized are Themistokles (*c.*470), Kimon (461), Thucydides son of Melesias (443), and Hyperbolus (417 or 416 or 415). After this, the practice seems to have fallen into disuse.

Several key points emerge. One, we can't be sure exactly why people were ostracized, although the known examples indicate that those ostracized were the losers in battles for political power. Two, archaeological finds of large numbers of sherds inscribed with one candidate's name by a single hand indicate that they were prepared beforehand. This suggests that campaigns were organized and that the institution was a political weapon. Three, the institution indicates that political argument was thought to centre very much on individuals. In the absence of parties, to get rid of a prominent individual was considered enough. There is no evidence to show a man's supporters were also penalized. Four, there is nevertheless some disagreement about the precise purpose of the institution. The concentration on individuals suggests it was part of the competitive *agon* of politics. However, some historians have gone further and seen it in a more sophisticated light as a positive check on the danger of tyranny, and on the concentration of power in the hands of one individual. The existence of a preliminary vote in the *ekklesia* does suggest it was perceived as some sort of safety valve and may thus have had an important role in permitting the development of the democracy.

Figure 30 A, B and C Ostraka with the names of (a) and (b) Themistokles and (c) Pericles. Fifth century BCE.

ST 2(b) contains an extract from an attack on Alcibiades, from a speech sometimes attributed to Andokides. The date is about 417 and the occasion may have been an ostracism. Note the combination of political and social abuse.

2 *Graphe paranomon*

A *graphe* was the name given in Athenian law to a public case (a private one was usually called a *dike*). A *graphe paranomon* was a prosecution alleging that a defendant had proposed in the *boule* or *ekklesia* a law or decree which was contrary to an existing law in form or content. The proposal, whether already voted on or not, was suspended until the prosecution had been heard in a law-court. If the jury found against the proposer, his proposal was annulled and he was fined. However, three convictions for this offence entailed *atimia*. After a law had been in force for a year, its proposer could no longer be prosecuted but the law itself could be annulled. The involvement of both *ekklesia* and courts in the procedure shows how questions of legality entailed a political de-cision. An example of prosecution under this heading is known from 415 (Speusippus, in Andokides 1.7) although the provision may have been institu-ted earlier. Also Plutarch refers to the prosecution of Demosthenes the *strategos* at about the same time (*Moralia*, 833d), and there are a number of examples from the fourth century indicating that the procedure became well established. Essentially it was a way of permitting the Assembly to change its mind. Such a safeguard implicitly recognizes the power of the orators to achieve questionable decisions. However, the *graphe paranomon* could be and was used as a political weapon.

Note the discussion of graphai *and the role of the sycophants in* WA 5.63.

The fact that prosecution could be initiated by 'anyone who wishes' gave a role to the 'hangers-on' of the main politicians and to those seeking financial gain. The extract from Aristophanes quoted in *WA* includes a reference to the *polypragmones* in the pejorative sense.

3 *Euthuna*

This was the examination of accounts which took place at the end of the term of office of state officials (see *WA* 5.32, 5.67). After the audit, a period of 30 days was allowed for the bringing of complaints against the outgoing officials. Thus, quite apart from questions of honesty, the *euthuna* could be used to raise questions of competence or broader political disputes. The Aristotelian *Con-stitution of Athens* 27 says that Pericles 'had first became prominent as a young man when he prosecuted Kimon at his *euthuna* as *strategos*' (*ST* 6).

It is also true that there were other dangers for prominent politicians than the due processes of law. Ephialtes (461) and Androkles (411) were assassinated. Kleon and Nikias were killed in or after military action. Theramenes was judicially killed (*WA* H.I.57).

6.5.3 Changes in political activity in the fifth century

> A kind of persuasion lived in his lips.
> He cast a spell on us.
> He was the only orator
> Who left his sting behind in his audience.

> (Eupolis fr.94.K)

The extract is from a fragment from an Old Comedy, *The Demes* by Eupolis. The orator referred to is Pericles. The passage is an interesting counterpart to the emphasis placed by Thucydides (for example, in 2.65) where he contrasts Pericles with the 'demagogues' who came after him. The truth is, of course, that in the developed democracy when crucial decisions were made in the Assembly, *any* ambitious politician had to be an effective speaker in order to influence decision-making by getting the majority vote. In fact, Thucydides did not actually use the word 'demagogue' in 2.65. What he says is that the sucessors of Pericles, because they were more on a level with one another, had to compete at 'pleasing the *demos*' in order to achieve their 'success'. The implication is that what they therefore lacked was consistency in policy. Thucydides does, however, use the word 'demagogue' elsewhere, with specific reference to Kleon (*aner demagogos* Book 4.20.3) and Androkles (Book 8.65.3).

In fact, as M.I. Finley pointed out in his influential article on this subject ('Athenian Demagogues', *Past and Present*, no. 21, 1962), the reference to demagogues in sources such as ?Aristotle *Constitution of Athens* 25 (*ST* 6) and Aristophanes combine a number of strands of meaning, the most important being implicit recognition of the *means* used by political leaders under the developed democracy, and anti-democratic distaste for the policies and personalities of some of the individual leaders. Finley points out the contradiction experienced by historians who are over-influenced by the bias of the Greek political writers – 'We cannot have it both ways: we cannot praise and admire the achievement of two centuries and at the same time dismiss the demagogues who were the architects of the political framework and the makers of policy, or the Assembly in and through which they did their work' (ibid.). *WA* 5.21 addresses this problem (somewhat obliquely).

Finley's article is included in The Offprints and you should read it in conjunction with your work on this section.

Another influential study of this general area tries to get round the difficulty by referring to *The New Politicians of Fifth Century Athens* (W. Robert Connor, Princeton, 1971). Connor shows how the change in methods required from the politician comes with development of the full democracy rather than after the death of Pericles.

To assess the degree of tension and change associated with the new politicians, we need to return to the basic questions of this section – how did the ambitious politician make his way and what did he have to do to maintain his position? The brief answer is that after the development of the full democracy, political decision-making took place in the council, the *ekklesia* and the jury courts, and the successful politician had to achieve majority support in these. Therefore the ability to speak effectively took on much greater importance and was more decisive than a reputation based on noble birth or military prowess, although these were still useful. From mid-century the demand for education and training in political skills attracted distinguished teachers to Athens. These teachers (sophists) introduced a broad range of ideas, but central to the demand for them was the desire to achieve excellence in argument and rhetoric.

Please read WA 4.43–8 and 7.20–1.

WA suggests something of their influence. You can also see, from the exploration of the generation gap in Aristophanes' *The Clouds*, some ways in which sophists might be said to have challenged traditional orthodoxy in education, politics, and natural and moral philosophy. These are issues which are relevant to Sections 7 and 8 of this block and will be investigated in more detail in Block 5.

Acquisition of the political skills appropriate to leadership in the democracy required money and leisure. The prominent men might not necessarily any longer be from aristocratic backgrounds but they were wealthy. (Compare the discussion in Part 1 Section 4 of this block about the wealth of, for example, Kleon and Nikias.) Detailed comparison of the financial and social background of prominent politicians with the presentation of them in comedy suggests that comedy tells us more about attitudes to social change and political competition than about the historical facts connected with these men.

Changes during the fifth century in the means necessary to *seek* prominence were therefore inevitably accompanied by changes in intellectual outlook and social values. The means necessary to *achieve* and *maintain* prominence were similarly not self-limiting. Because the democracy was *direct*, leadership had constantly to be re-assessed and could be challenged at any time. Policy could be subject to crowd psychology exacerbated by urban concentration in time of war. That is of course only one side of the question. The other side is that most of those who manned the ships and fought the battles, and some of those who created the buildings, were involved in the decisions made about them: 'power is in the hands not of a minority but of the whole people' (Thucydides, 2.37) and it is this which notably underlies the distaste evident in the anti-democratic writers. We should remember that not all the business of the Assembly concerned sending expeditions to Sicily and the like. Political skills included competent management of resources as well as rhetoric. Nevertheless, it is true that the developed democracy created its orators (*rhetores*), and the competing *rhetores* in turn created expectations and manipulated debate. Structurally there was a two-way relationship between *rhetor* and *demos*, the tendencies of which can be seen in the change in emphasis away from ostracism of the individual and towards use of the *graphe paranomon* as an attempt to confront the problem of continuity and stability in the political and legal framework.

The demagogues have sometimes been described as *underminers* of the sovereignty of the *demos*, because of the political and manipulative skills they exercised. An opposing view, emphasizing the basis of the power of the *demos*, has been put by M.I. Finley:

> The *demos* recognized the instrumental role of political rights and were more concerned in the end with the substantive decisions through their power to select, dismiss and punish their political leaders. On this score they were favoured by an impartial and genuine equality – equality to vote.
>
> ('The freedom of the citizen in the Greek world', *Talenta*, 7, 1970, pp.1–23)

It would be useful to consider arguments for and against each of these positions – you might like to do this in a tutorial or self-help group.

Before going on to the next section, please look back to the themes and questions raised at the end of Section 5 of this block and update your notes. From your work on the articles included in The Offprints, you will now be very aware of the way in which the evidence used to discuss one topic can often inform another. You will also have discovered how the different approaches of modern scholars can lead to fierce debate about interpretation of evidence and the conclusions to be drawn! Now is your chance to reflect upon some of these key issues for yourself.

6.6 Further Reading

BLUNDELL, S. (1995) *Women in Ancient Greece*, British Museum Press.

CARTER, L.B. (1986) *The Quiet Athenian*, Oxford University Press.

CARTLEDGE, P. (1993) *The Greeks*, Oxford University Press.

FISHER, N.R.E. (ed.) (1976) *Social Values in Classical Athens*, Dent; this includes an excellent introductory essay and translated extracts from the orators, comedy and inscriptions.

HORNBLOWER, S. (1983) *The Greek World 479–323 BC*, Methuen; Chapters 2, 11, 12 and 13 contain discussion of themes raised in this section.

HORNBLOWER, S. and OSBORNE, R. (eds) (1994) *Ritual, Finance, Politics: democratic accounts rendered to D.M. Lewis*, Clarendon Press.

MCAUSLEN, I. and WALCOT, P. (eds) (1996) *Women in Antiquity*, Oxford University Press.

OSBORNE, R. (1985) *Demos: the discovery of Classical Attika*, Cambridge University Press.

SINCLAIR, R. (1988) *Democracy and Participation at Athens*, Cambridge University Press.

TODD, S. (1993) *The Shape of Athenian Law*, Clarendon Press.

7 CHALLENGES TO THE *NOMOI*

For this section you will need *WA*, the Supplementary Texts, Thucydides and (for 7.2) your Penguin edition of *The Last Days of Socrates*.

Nomos (pl. *nomoi*): law, custom, observance, habit. *Nomos* may include the idea of what is conventionally right or accepted.

7.1 The politics of piety

> In all this it was impossible to say whether those who suffered deserved their punishment or not, but it was quite clear that the rest of the city, as things were, benefited greatly.
>
> (Thucydides 6.60)

In this section we shall be looking at a series of related incidents which took place in Athens in 415. The incidents apparently involved religious offences, but the way in which they were treated and the effects on Athenian politics and on the conduct of the war raise a broad range of questions about the relationship between religion and politics in Athenian public life. Here we shall be examining the sources primarily from the political angle, but a number of the religious issues raised will be studied in more detail in Block 5 and in TV7.

7.1.1 Herms and Mysteries

In the early summer of 415 the Athenians, revived by the comparatively peaceful period following the peace of Nikias in 421, were preparing to launch the ambitious expedition to Sicily. It was important that military initiatives should take place at propitious times (see Thucydides 8.1 and 7.50). However, two incidents occurred which appeared ominous. First, Herms were mutilated. Herms were stone pillars, with carved head and erect phallus, which stood outside both private and public buildings to ward off ill-fortune (see Figure 31).

Such mutilation in any case amounted to sacrilege, and at a time of crucial public importance seemed to threaten the success of the expedition. In the second incident Alcibiades, who was one of the *strategoi* in charge of the expedition, was accused in the Assembly of taking part in a blasphemous parody of the Eleusinian Mysteries.

Please now look up the background in WA H.I.49, and then read Thucydides' account in Book 6.26–32, noticing especially how he places it just before his description of the elaborate public departure ceremony for the fleet, with its associated religious ritual. Look also at the TV Notes for TV7. Then consider what issues were involved. Did these go beyond the question of blasphemy? (In the discussion I shall add to the information you already have.)

Discussion _____

Clearly, yes. It was not just a question of mutilation and profanation being sacrilegious, but of *who* had done this and why.

So far as the Herms were concerned, the mutilation was interpreted as showing a desire by some group or individuals to bring ill-luck to the Sicilian Expedition, on which so many hopes rested. If the outrage had indeed been perpetrated by an aristocratic drinking club, this made the damage more serious because there would then be a suggestion of conspiracy (for the political aspects of these clubs, see Section 6.5.1 above). We know from a fragment of Lysias (fr.143) that one club, the *kakodaimonistai* (lit. evil spirits) was supposed to have deliberately chosen to dine on inauspicious days in order to flout superstition. However, to mutilate the Herms on the eve of the Expedition suggested something more sinister than mere disrespect for religious convention.

Figure 31 Sculptor carving a herm, mid-fifth century (Inv. nr. Chr. VIII 967).

Figure 32 Eleusis, Hall of the Mysteries; reconstruction of the sanctuary of Demeter and Persephone.

So far as the Mysteries were concerned, a number of important principles and traditions were involved. The Eleusinian Mysteries were perhaps unique in that they brought together in one set of rituals questions of personal behaviour and public, indeed pan-Hellenic, organization. Initiation into this long-established cult was by this time open to all Greek-speakers (including women and slaves) who could make the journey and afford the cost, and the small fortified town of Eleusis therefore attracted thousands of visitors. (Map 5 in the Course Guide shows its position.) However, in the context of our study of 415, it is the 'public face' of the Eleusinian Mysteries which is more important. During the early part of the century, responsibility for Eleusis had been removed from the aristocratic controllers (albeit with some face-saving concessions) and Eleusis had been integrated into the Athenian imperial network of financial and religious contributions. This is shown by an inscription recording the collection of the 'first fruits' for Eleusis and the detailed arrangements made both in the Attic *demes* and the allied cities:

> Those who take this action shall have many blessings, and rich and fruitful harvests, those who do no harm to the Athenians, the city of Athens or the two goddesses.

> (*ST* 17e)

When Eleusis was absorbed into Attica, the Athenians had clearly gained in prestige. In the sixth century the Peisistratids built a larger religious complex and this was further enhanced by Kimon and later Iktinos when commissioned by Pericles. The relationship was symbolically expressed in the great procession along the Sacred Way from Athens to Eleusis carrying the 'holy things of Demeter'. *The Frogs* of Aristophanes contains a sequence in which a chorus of Initiates of the Mysteries process in welcome to Dionysos' arrival in the underworld (lines 312ff.). However, it is the procession ritual which is parodied, not the initiation rites, which were supposed to be kept secret. In 416 when the Spartans invaded Attica, the land route for the procession was no longer safe and a sea route had to be taken. In 415, therefore, the Athens/Eleusis link was already a sensitive area. ◆

7.1.2 Status of the Eleusinian Mysteries

The importance of Eleusis as a symbol therefore spreads into a number of areas the Athenians held vital, and this accounts for the fact that profanation could be seen as a wider attack on the unity and well-being of the state and a questioning of the dignity of the role of Athens as the custodian of the rite.

Look again at the extract from the fourth-century document by Isokrates, Panegyricus *28–9 (ST 18(a)).*

Here the relationship between Athens and Demeter (who is identified with the basis of agriculture) is used as a model for enhancing the role of Athens in Hellenic agriculture and religion. (Compare the way in which Spartan invasion of Attica in 416 threatened agriculture both literally and symbolically in closing the normal processional route.)

Herodotus (6.75–84) records that when the Spartan king Kleomenes went mad and killed himself in the early years of the fifth century, the Athenians attributed this to divine punishment because he had attacked Eleusis and devastated groves sacred to Demeter and Kore. Herodotus also says that it was only the Athenians who produced this theory; other states attributed the events to other blasphemies. Thus Herodotus' anecdote is further evidence for the importance placed by the Athenians on Eleusis. Taken together, the Herodotus and Isokrates references indicate that this extended over the whole century which we are studying. Xenophon records that in 403, after the battle for the Piraeus, the herald of the Eleusinian initiates made a plea for reconciliation to those who had fought for the Thirty Tyrants:

> Fellow citizens, why are you driving us out of the city? Why do you want to kill us? We have never done you any harm. We have shared with you in the most holy religious services, the sacrifices and in splendid festivals ... in the names of the gods of our fathers and mothers, of the bonds of kinship and marriage and friendship which are shared by so many of us on both sides, I beg you to feel some shame in front of gods and men and to give up this sin against your fatherland.

> (Xenophon, *Hellenica,* 2.4 20–1, tr. R. Warner)

Figure 33 Eleusis, view of part of the Hall of Mysteries (see site plan in Broadcast Notes, TV7).

Figure 34, A, B, C Scene from an attic red figure hydria of the fourth century. Persephone (Kore), crowned with laurel and carrying two torches, stands between Demeter and Dionysos, who is sitting on an omphalos and holding a thyrsus. Compare the Triptolemos relief (Illustration Booklet I.72) in which the boy representing the Athenian people receives the gift of corn from Demeter and Kore. The reconstruction of the scene (C), by Adolf Furtwaengler and Carl Reichhold, involved some restoration (Griechische Vasenmalerei 1900, Munich).

Xenophon emphasizes an important aspect of the status of the Mysteries and religious observance generally, namely the role of religion as part of the network of shared experiences which helped to unify the community and could therefore serve as a basis for political appeals. The evidence from Herodotus, Xenophon, Isokrates and the First-Fruits inscription makes it clear that we cannot draw any clear distinction between the secular and sacred status of Eleusis. The two run with one another, perhaps never more so than in 415.

7.1.3 Causes and effects of the accusation

Turn to ST 2(a) and read the extract from Andokides, 'On the Mysteries' 11–13, comparing this account with Thucydides 6.28 and 6.60–1.

Discussion ⎯⎯⎯⎯⎯⎯⎯⎯⎯⎯⎯⎯⎯⎯⎯⎯⎯⎯⎯⎯⎯⎯⎯⎯

According to Andokides, the accusation against Alcibiades was made in the Assembly. This indicates that political concerns were paramount. Andokides was writing in his own defence, some 16 years later, a little after Thucydides. (For the circumstances, see introduction to *ST 2*.) Andokides' speech is concerned with trying to establish his own innocence, but it does give useful information on the supposed sequence of events. Thucydides is less concerned with trying to present what actually happened. His interest is in what was thought to have happened and the effects of public concern. His account in 6.60–1 makes it clear that, at the time, the Athenians were sensitive to the possibility of conspiracy against the democracy by Spartan sympathizers and by oligarchs in Argos, Alcibiades being possibly linked with both. Of course, we have to bear in mind that one of Thucydides' primary interests in analysing political events in Athens is the role of factional strife, real or imagined, and this interest governs his treatment here. We also have indicators elsewhere in Thucydides (for example, 2.54) that he considered superstition increased at times of crisis. In the context of a plot against the democracy, however, a mock celebration of the Mysteries need not have implied parody; it might have involved the use of the Mysteries to sanction an oath-taking ceremony among the conspirators.

Whatever the exact nature of the 'profanation', and whether Alcibiades was involved or not, it seems most likely that the accusation against him was promoted most vigorously by his political enemies amid a general context of public fear of conspiracy. It is clear from the sources that the incidents were taken very seriously. Prosopographical research has revealed the names of some 68 men, known to have been charged or informed against for either or both of the Herms and Mysteries incidents (*HCT*, vol.IV, pp.276–80) and there were at least 28 others whose names are not known. Of those whose fate is known, a large proportion fled or were executed. There is inscriptional evidence from the *stelai* recording the sale of the goods of those who were convicted, that wealthy men were among them (see *ST* 17(c) and illustration in *WA* 5.13). The vigour with which the prosecutions were undertaken is demonstrated by the fact that Alcibiades thought it wisest not to return to stand trial. You will get the chance in the next section to look in more detail at his subsequent actions, but clearly the incident and its aftermath deprived the Athenians of one of their foremost commanders at a crucial stage in the Sicilian venture, and precipitated his collaboration with the Spartans afterwards.

What conclusions can be drawn from these incidents? Firstly, the mutilation of the Herms (whoever the perpetrators were) does provide evidence that respect for traditional religious forms was not universal. But that on its own is hardly startling. There is a lot more detailed evidence from comedy to show that parody of features of religious observance does not necessarily undermine the principle, while in Block 5 we will look at the rational and scientific studies which were thought by some to undermine traditional observance in a different way.

Secondly, and more important, is that apparent impiety could be presented as threatening the *nomoi*, the written and unwritten laws of constitution and behaviour to which Pericles was made to refer in Thucydides 2.37. This is the means by which impiety can be said to be a political act, and a religious charge becomes a political weapon. Sir Kenneth Dover has commented to me that 'there is another aspect of the matter too; the city sacrifices to gods, and the gods welcome that; if the city is impoverished or depopulated, the gods are hurt by the lack of sacrifices. Hence any allegedly unpatriotic act can be called impious.'

According to later sources, the last third of the fifth century saw a series of trials, as least some of which had political undertones. In Block 5 you will be studying the trial and condemnation of Socrates on religious/political charges. It may well be that the concern of later sources with impiety trials reflects the influence in antiquity of the example of Socrates. In the absence of contemporary evidence, it is a matter of speculation as to how far other examples of trials on religious charges are evidence of the sensitivity of the Athenians to implied or actual challenge to the established network of religious, social and political traditions. In some cases they may also indicate the utility of the religious charge as a political weapon. 415 is important because we have strong evidence about what was said to have occurred. Our problem is to adduce reasons. What is unprecedented in 415 is the extent of the public concern and the numbers investigated or charged.

Thucydides presents the charges as very much a kind of communal release of fear and tension (6.61). You might like to consider the extent to which the events of 415 provide evidence through which we can question any of the claims made in the Funeral Speech in Thucydides.

Look back to Questions 4 and 7 in Section 5.3.2 of this block.

The speech itself is significantly lacking in direct treatment of religious issues. Apart from the brief reference to festivals at 2.38, the most relevant passage is at 2.37 with its reference to obedience to the *nomoi*, written or unwritten, in public life. The ideas of the 30s and 20s which you will be studying in the next block suggest there was less of a consensus about the *nomoi* than Pericles is made to claim. The events of 415 perhaps suggest that this was reflected in political as well as intellectual uncertainty. ◆

Further Reading

BURKERT, W. (1985) *Greek Religion*, Blackwell; Chapters 6 and 7.

EASTERLING, P.E. and MUIR, J.V. (eds) (1985) *Greek Religion & Society*, Cambridge University Press.

LEWIS, D.M. (1966) 'After the profanation of the Mysteries', *Ancient Society & Institutions* (studies presented to Victor Ehrenberg), Blackwell.

PARKER, R. (1996) *Athenian Religion*, Clarendon Press.

PRITCHETT, W. (1953) 'The Attic *Stelai*', *Hesperia* 22, pp.225ff.

7.2 The individual and the *polis*

> But I do know that to do wrong and to disobey my superior, whether God or man, is bad and dishonourable.
>
> (Socrates in Plato, *Apology*, 29b, Penguin translation, p.52)

In this section we are going to look at the concept of civic obligation. We have considered in previous sections the network of obligations which citizens had towards themselves, their families and close associates, as well as the implications of participation in public affairs. We saw in one interpretation of the Funeral Speech in Thucydides that there is some evidence of a tension between these obligations and the desire to maintain social and political unity in the *polis*.

To open up this problem I want to look in detail at one of Plato's earlier dialogues, *Crito*. The date of composition of the dialogue (it has to be after 399) strictly takes it outside our period, but the fact that it is based on the experiences and ideas of the historical Socrates gives it an immediate relevance to the tensions in politics and moral ideas which emerged towards the end of the fifth century.

In Block 5 you will be studying Socrates in detail, including the underlying reasons for his trial and execution in 399. Plato devoted a major work, the *Apology*, to an account of the trial. At this stage, therefore, we shall not be concerning ourselves with the trial itself or the origins of the charges laid against Socrates. All you need to know is that he was tried and condemned (on charges of refusing to recognize the gods of the state and introducing other new gods, and of corrupting the youth) and that some of his associates, notably Plato and Xenophon, produced more or less historical accounts, designed to clear Socrates for posterity and disseminate his ideas (Socrates himself wrote nothing). There are quite a lot of references to Socrates in the index of *WA*, and you might like to look them up so that you have background information about a) his life as a citizen, b) his associates and pupils, c) the reaction to him during the last quarter of the fifth century (and especially his portrayal by Aristophanes in *The Clouds*, which you will be studying in Block 5). However, it is not essential to do this if you are short of time, since there is also relevant information in the introduction to the Penguin text (although the portrait of Socrates there is arguably somewhat idealized). TV6 considers the material evidence for the historical context.

Then turn to Plato, *Crito* (Penguin text, p.76). The translator's note on pp.71–5 gives the context. Note that the 'stage directions' are not present in the original manuscript. The issue with which we are concerned here is the decision by Socrates not to take advantage of the opportunity to escape (made available by the delay before his execution) and especially the reasons for and against the decision as put forward in the dialogue by Socrates and his friend Crito.

I suggest you now read the dialogue straight through to get the feel of the shape and to enjoy the humour and irony which are a feature of Plato's presentation of Socrates. Then read through a second time, more slowly, noting down the main features of the argument:

1   *Why does Crito think Socrates should escape? To what values and loyalties does he appeal in order to try to persuade him?*

2   *What are Socrates' reasons for remaining? To what values and loyalties does he appeal in order to try to persuade Crito?*

Discussion

1   Crito's views

The main statement of Crito's views is on pp.77–80. Thereafter, he becomes the foil for Socrates' rebuttal of the arguments he has put forward.

Crito makes it clear that he is speaking as a friend of Socrates. On p.78 he is said to be a friend. Friendship, of course, is double-edged and goes hand in hand with concern for his own reputation. He is concerned that 'popular opinion' (*doxa*) will think that he has neglected his own duty as Socrates' friend by not saving him, and that he himself may be accused of being miserly (p.78). Notice especially that Crito thinks that popular opinion will not even imagine that Socrates might *refuse* to escape. It will automatically blame Crito for not supporting his friend.

Crito also adds the point that Socrates does not need to worry about the punishment to be meted out to those arranging his escape (pp.78–9). The risk of a fine or confiscation of property is worth it (and by implication has to be *seen* to be worth it: cf. the point about the cost of arranging the escape, p.78). Crito is presented as having a low opinion of the informers (*sycophantes*) who will need to be bribed, and perhaps too of the foreigners who are so willing to make their money available. He also emphasizes that Socrates will be welcomed and looked after if he leaves Attica for another *polis*. The example of Thessaly perhaps indicates Crito's oligarchic sympathies (or Socrates'?).

The final plank in Crito's argument is that Socrates has already cast doubt on the reputation of his friends by allowing himself to be condemned in the first place. The references on pp.78–80 are to the fact that Socrates could have fled before his trial or at least conducted his defence more positively (see *Apology*, pp.61–2 for the alternative 'punishment' put forward to the jury by Socrates). Therefore, argues Crito, Socrates positively owes it to his friends to escape and to free them from the threat to their reputation entailed by appearing to allow him to die. The 'disgrace' (*aischra*) to which Crito refers (p.80) is for Socrates' friends as much as for the man himself.

In summary, Crito's appeal is to *philia* (friendship) in conjunction with *time* (reputation). In escaping, Socrates would protect the reputation of his friends from the accusations of public opinion (*doxa*) that they had been mean with their money or lacked courage or resourcefulness. There is a nice irony in that Crito is presented as appealing to the condemned Socrates to safeguard his, Crito's, reputation. As we saw earlier in this block, the network of friendship and reputation was indeed a closely interwoven one and a glance at the action taken by other condemned men indicates that escape was an expected reaction.

2 *Socrates' reply*

Socrates' reply is more complicated and falls into several distinct sections. I expect you noticed the way in which he undermined Crito's argument by the use of leading questions to show up (to create?) inconsistencies in Crito's position and to persuade Crito to acknowledge these. In Block 5 you will be considering Socratic method in more detail, so here we will concentrate on what Socrates is saying rather than the way in which he arrives at his conclusions.

In the initial part of the discussion (pp.80–83) Socrates takes up the point Crito has made about 'what people will think' and tries to show that no attention should be paid to 'the advice of the many who have no expert knowledge' (p.82). Not everyone's opinion has equal status and, according to Socrates, just as opinion on medical matters is valued only when it comes from a doctor, so advice on moral actions, just or unjust (*dikaion* or *adikon*), honourable or dishonourable (*kalon* or *aischron*), good or bad (*agathon* or *kakon*), should be valued when it comes from someone with expert knowledge and not when it reflects the opinions of the many. The doctrine of the expert is a regular and important feature of Plato's dialogues. The anti-democratic implications are obvious. Notice, too, that on pp.83–4 Socrates specifically links the question of the opinions of the ordinary people with the pre-eminence of ideas about reputation. In fact, as you saw in Section 6, the primacy of reputation was no respecter of classes and was as much a feature of aristocratic discourse as of popular values (in fact it originated in the heroic/aristocratic ethos). The rejection of reputation as a criterion for 'moral' judgements is an important challenge to prevailing values.

A second important challenge comes in the section on pp.84–5. Here Socrates argues that restraining oneself from wrong-doing includes abstaining from injuring one's enemies and from returning evil for evil. Of course this cuts straight across the convention (linked with reputation) that it was praiseworthy to harm one's enemies (see *WA* Chapter 3). This step in the argument allows Socrates to hold that even though the (democratic) *polis* has harmed him and acted unjustly towards him, he is not entitled to return the harm done.

Next (pp.85–92) Socrates puts an imaginary argument on behalf of the Laws and Constitution of Athens. (Note that where your translation has Laws, the text has *nomoi*; we are still dealing with the language of *Antigone* and the Funeral Speech.) His arguments are really of two kinds, as discussed overleaf.

First, he maintains that if the laws of the city are challenged by private individuals, then chaos will ensue. (Consider the use of 'turned upside down' in the middle of p.86. The Greek word used is one which can also refer to the capsizing of ships – cf. the image of the ship of state used in *Antigone*.) Compare also the claim attributed to Kleon in Thucydides 3.37:

> We should realize that a city is better off with bad laws, so long as they remained fixed, than with good laws which are constantly being altered ...

However, the conclusion that Kleon is made to draw – 'that as a general rule states are better governed by the man in the street than by intellectuals' – is diametrically opposed to Plato's.

Secondly, Socrates seeks to show that he has voluntarily remained in the Athenian *polis*, benefiting from its education, civic organization and legal system and social values, and would therefore be betraying precisely those values if he now left. This argument is closely related to that of personal consistency. Socrates was supposed to have claimed in his teaching (and at his trial) that 'goodness and justice, institutions and laws are the most precious possessions of mankind' (p.90). The Laws are made to suggest that, if he left, Socrates would in some sense become *foreign* (p.91). The fact that the laws of his native *polis* have been misused is no just reason for rejecting them. ◆

In some of his other works (notably *Gorgias* and *The Republic*) Plato returns to the themes raised in the last part of *Crito* and puts forward his plan for ensuring that laws can be both stable *and* good *and* decided by (moral) experts. In *Crito*, Plato is not merely attacking the notion that popular opinion may be an arbiter of morality; he is also, through Socrates, questioning the network of established values with reputation at its core. In using the wealthy traditionalist Crito as an example, he makes it clear that it is a whole system of values he is questioning and not just the misconceived actions of the restored democracy. In assessing the relevance of *Crito* as a source for a discussion of the question of the relationship between the individual and the state, we therefore run up against a number of problems:

1   The dialogue was written in response to a historical situation, the condemnation of Socrates.

2   Nevertheless, there are clear indications that the subject-matter does not only respond to a historical situation but also marks a stage in the development of Plato's ideas about the criteria for moral values and the genesis of just laws in Athenian society.

3   Is there a danger that we might reason back from (2) to (1), and thus attribute to the historical Socrates and to Athenian discourse generally in the late fifth century, ideas which are really only developed by Plato in the early fourth century as his own radical response to the problems he had witnessed?

4   The dialogue also raises questions about old age and immortality which we have not pursued here.

I am certainly not going to attempt a detailed response to those problems at this point. But I would like you to bear them in mind as you work through the rest of this block and the next one.

TV6 presents some of the material evidence relevant to study of the historical Socrates and the way in which Plato presents him. But we also have evidence available in other sources. For example, Aristotle (*Rhetoric*, III.23.1398 and 24) says that Socrates declined an invitation to the court of Archelaos, where Euripides and others did go (see *Crito*, p.79). Nearer to Socrates' time we also have interesting material in the *Memorabilia* of Xenophon, written as part of the tradition of apology for Socrates. There is an important sequence in Book 3 in which Xenophon depicts Socrates conversing with Pericles about the decline of Athens and the envy and litigiousness of the citizens. Here, too, Socrates is made to put forward a version of the doctrine of the expert.

We shall return to these and similar questions in the Revision Block. In the meantime, look back at Section 5.3.2 of this block and consider whether *Crito* offers useful evidence in relation to any of the themes and questions raised.

7.3 Cassette Lecture 3: 'State and individual in Athens, 508–450 BC'

In this lecture, on Cassette 10, Band 1, Simon Hornblower takes up themes relevant to Sections 5, 6 and 7 of this block. Please listen to it before reading further, and think about the points raised in the discussion and cassette notes.

7.4 Further Reading

DOVER, K. (1974) *Greek Popular Morality*, Blackwell; Section VI, 'Priorities', is particularly relevant.

WOOZLEY, A.D. (1979) *The Arguments of Plato's Crito*, Duckworth; Woozley claims that the arguments attributed to Socrates about why it is wrong to break the law are bad but interesting.

8 EURIPIDES, *THE WOMEN OF TROY*

Study guide

For this section you will need your set text, Euripides' *The Women of Troy*, in Euripides, *The Bacchae and other plays*, tr. P. Vellacott (Penguin).

You should also listen to Cassette 3, Band 4 as directed.

8.1 Introduction

Commentators, both ancient and modern, tend to disagree about Euripides, sometimes violently. In his play *The Frogs* (which won first prize in the Lenaia in 405), Aristophanes introduces a debate about the respective merits of Aeschylus and Euripides. (The context involved possible recall of one of the two from the underworld. Sophocles had recently died and was not included.) Aeschylus had been dead for fifty years, so the debate drew on his reputation and the way in which he was identified (rightly or wrongly) with the civic morality associated with victory in the Persian Wars. Euripides (d.406) had first taken part in a dramatic festival in 455. Through the debate in *The Frogs*, Aristophanes presents the idea that Euripides had debased traditional values by introducing into tragedy the ordinary and the sceptical, and by provoking questioning and dissent about morality, religion and the heroic status of the tragic protagonist.

Now, we cannot say that the issues explored by Aristophanes in a dramatic context necessarily represent his own views, any more than we can attribute to Euripides a didactic 'message' expressed in his plays. It is enough that a contrast can be drawn between the 'traditionalist' interpretation of Aeschylus and the differing subject-matter and dramatic approach of Euripides, and that the contrast was thought to be a matter of public interest. Euripides is often said to have intellectualized tragic drama, to have overworked the techniques of sophistic debate (see, for example, Ruth Scodel's comments on the 'dry and analytic rhetoric' in *The Trojan Trilogy of Euripides*, 1980, Chapter 1). Yet Aristotle called him 'the most tragic of the poets' (*Poetics*, 1453a 30). Clearly, therefore, we are dealing with problems of range and diversity in Euripides *and* in the judgements made about his work.

If you read the introduction by Vellacott to the Penguin edition of *The Women of Troy* (it is not essential to do so), you will see that the translator's discussion of the play rests on two main assertions. The first is that the play is static, lacking action, plot and movement in the dialogue. The second is that the play is somehow best understood in the context of the immediate political situation in Athens – the recent reduction of Melos (in 416, and see Thucydides 5.116) and the imminence of the Sicilian Expedition are specifically mentioned. In my discussion of the play, I shall try to suggest that the first of these suggestions is untrue and the second both misleading and limiting.

Vellacott's introduction does, however, make one useful point, that the treatment of suffering in the play does 'stir the conscience and fears of our own century'. The questions we want to ask of the play and our emotional response may be mediated to a significant degree by the concepts and perceptions of our own age. This does not matter as long as we are aware of it. Some modern versions have, for example, emphasized the political context, setting it in Vietnam or in Algeria during the crisis which accompanied the ending of French domination (Jean-Paul Sartre's 1966 adaptation, *Les Troyennes*). It is no bad thing to have a sense of the immediacy to our own century of the issues raised. You saw earlier in the course how Tom Paulin's 'version' of Prometheus grafted a twentieth-century response onto ideas suggested by the Greek author.

However, the way in to the play which I am going to suggest here is adapted to the needs of our main aim in this block, the study of tensions and change in fifth-century Athens. We will, therefore, be looking for ways in which Euripides implicitly supports or questions civic, religious and moral conventions; the way in which he uses and adapts the shared framework of mythological and Homeric reference; and the way in which he presents and evaluates the past (in this case the Greek heroes of the Trojan Wars). We will be thinking about the possible relationship between this use of the past and his shaping of the way his audience might look at the present.

Thus, in a sense we are using Euripides' play as a historical source. But a play is not a source in the same way that Thucydides is. It is not, for instance, written to record information, nor to present a specific argued-out interpretation of what has happened. The value of drama as a historical source is the indirect evidence it yields about the issues and ideas which were of concern at the time it was written and the way these were perceived and explored. Therefore, we are going to approach *The Women of Troy* first and foremost as an example of its own genre. In a moment I will ask you to do a first general reading of the play with special reference to its structure and the relationship between the form of the play and the issues Euripides raises. Then you will be asked to do an interactive cassette exercise relating your reading of the play to your earlier work on Greek drama. When you return to the block we will be looking in detail at the way in which certain important themes in the language and ideas in the play are presented and explored by Euripides. These will include the relationship between gods and humans, agents and victims; the interplay between emotion and intellect in Euripides' choice of issues and language; patterns of reference in image and situation; and the implications of the centrality of the female characters. To help you with your initial reading, I have included below a breakdown of the basic structure of the play and a note on the context given by other plays in the trilogy.

8.2 Context of the trilogy

The Women of Troy was produced in 415 and won second prize at the Great Dionysia. It was the third play in a trilogy. The two preceding plays were the *Alexandros* and the *Palamedes*. The accompanying satyr play was *Sisyphus*. Only fragments of these plays survive, but in the case of *Alexandros* they are quite extensive (Alexandros = Paris). The *Alexandros* starts with the disobedience of Hecabe and Priam to the oracle of Apollo which forbade them to rear Paris on the grounds that he would be 'the destruction of Troy and the ruin of Pergamum'. The action covers Paris' career before the abduction of Helen. It thus informs the debate about responsibility in the Third Episode of *The Women of Troy*. In the *Alexandros*, Cassandra is used to prophesy the future and also mentions a number of incidents which are drawn on in *The Women of Troy*, notably the judgement of Paris, the death of Hector and the Wooden Horse.

The *Palamedes* opens the way for the vilification of Odysseus by showing his role in the condemnation by the Greeks outside Troy of one of their men, the wise Palamedes, who was innocent and only condemned by false evidence planted by Odysseus.

Shirley Barlow has described the plots of the first two plays as those of 'action' and 'intrigue' respectively (Aris and Phillips, p.30; see 'Further Reading' at the end of Section 8).

8.3 Structure

When you read, I suggest you make short notes on the way Euripides uses different aspects of the structure for lyric, narrative, debate and so on. Notice the occurrence of the single set speech (the technical term is *rhesis*), debate (the technical term *agon* emphasizes the competitive element in the encounter between two speakers), *stichomythia* (one-line dialogue), and the way these spoken parts are differentiated in your text. Look out also for the choral odes – the *parodos* marks the Chorus' first entrance while the *stasimon* or short choral ode stands between the spoken episodes.

The play can be broken down as follows:

Prologue	Poseidon and Athena lines 1–92 (Penguin, pp.89–93)
Hecabe's monody (lyric song)	lines 93–150 (pp.93–4)
Parodos	lines 151–235 (pp.94–7)
First episode	Hecabe and Cassandra (with Talthybius) lines 236–514 (pp.97–107)
First stasimon	lines 515–564 (pp.107–8)
Second episode	Hecabe and Andromache (with Talthybius) lines 565–796 (pp.108–116)
Second stasimon	lines 797–856 (pp.116–8)
Third episode (agon)	Hecabe and Helen (with Menelaus) lines 856–1059 (pp.118–24)
Third stasimon	lines 1060–1127 (pp.124–6)
Fourth episode (Exodos)	Hecabe and the Trojan Women (with Talthybius) lines 1123–1332 (pp.126–33)

8.4 First reading and audio-cassette exercise

INTERACTIVE

Now read through The Women of Troy, *and see how Euripides explores a theme, not of 'action' or 'intrigue' but of suffering. After this first reading of the play, turn to Cassette 3, Band 4, 'An introduction to Euripides' The Women of Troy', and work through the discussion and exercises on the cassette and in the accompanying notes before returning to the block.*

8.5 Gods and humans

Two gods, Poseidon and Athene, figure in the brief opening scene of the play. Poseidon, the god of the sea, is supposed to have been associated especially with Troy, and the audience takes for granted Athene's association with the Greeks and the part she has played in promoting their victory. The structural importance of the scene is three-fold. Firstly, the gods relate the play to the context (previously known from myth and from Homer) of the vicissitudes which the Greeks are to suffer during their return from Asia Minor to Greece. Secondly, they introduce and explain some of the central religious and moral issues in the play. Thirdly, they are used by Euripides to emphasize the separateness of gods and humans. The Prologue is not primarily concerned with rivalry among the gods, nor with their alliances with opposing factions of humans. Something has happened to unite the two gods. It is not the mere fact of the ending of war, of defeat for one state, which has done this. Poseidon was and remains a Trojan god – 'Troy and its people were my city ... and my affection has not faded' (lines 3–4). He is, in a sense, defeated himself:

> Athene, and Hera of Argos, the gods who joined in league
> To achieve this end, have worsted me: now I must leave
> Ilion the famous, leave my altars. When desolation
> Falls like a blight, the day for the worship of gods is past.

(lines 21–4)

Yet Athene is far from triumphant. Her aim is to enlist from Poseidon 'your powerful aid and alliance on behalf of Troy' (lines 60–1). Making the homeward voyage disastrous for the Greeks is seen by Athene as in some sense redressing the balance for Troy. The reason for Athene's change of attitude is that the Greeks have behaved blasphemously in victory. She cites the dragging of Cassandra from sanctuary at Athene's shrine and her rape by Aias. Poseidon has already referred to the killing of Priam on the altar steps of Zeus the Protector (line 16). This was a particularly ironic blasphemy since it was precisely the power of this god which was supposed to protect suppliants. Poseidon also refers to the subsequent fate of Cassandra:

> ... whom Apollo himself left virgin – she
> Will be taken by force, in contempt of the god and all pious feeling
> By King Agamemnon as his concubine.

(lines 36–8)

It is important to note that the gods are not presented as themselves recoiling from the destruction of the city and the treatment meted out to the defeated as such. Their specific objection is religious and their aim:

> that Greeks may learn in future
> To respect my altars and show humility before the gods.

(lines 82–3)

Poseidon makes the application clear:

> When a man who takes a city includes in the general destruction
> Temples of the high gods and tombs that honour the dead,
> He is a fool: his own destruction follows him close.

(lines 90–2)

Think back for a moment to your reading of Aeschylus' *The Persians* in Block 1, Section 6. Do you remember how the Chorus of Persian Elders was made by Aeschylus to attribute to Zeus the crucial role in bringing about the defeat of Xerxes?

> Thy hand, O Zeus our king, has swept from sight
> The boastful pride of Persia's vast array,
> And veiled the sheets of Susa
> In gloomy mists of mourning.

(lines 533–6).

Later in the play the ghost of Darius, the previous king and father of Xerxes, explains (anachronistically) the reason for Zeus' hostility to the Persians:

> .... Zeus, throned on high
> Sternly chastises arrogant and boastful men.

(828–9)

> Marching through Hellas, without scruple they destroyed
> Statues of gods, burned temples; levelled with the ground
> Altars and holy precincts, now one heap of rubble.
> Therefore then sacrilege is matched in suffering
> And more will follow; for the well-spring of their path
> Is not yet dry; soon new disaster gushes forth.

(lines 810–15)

Aeschylus was adding a religious sanction to his celebration of the victory of Greeks over Persians. But notice how those defending their own territory have a built-in religious 'advantage'. They defend their hearths, gods and temples (see *Women of Troy*, 386ff.). If these are destroyed, the invader may incur the wrath of the gods. But is it possible to achieve victory without such destruction (compare Thucydides 2.39)? The dividing line between material/secular and spiritual/psychological outrage cannot always be clearly defined, as we shall see on returning to Euripides.

The fact that Euripides sets out two aspects to the gods' involvement in the Prologue does, I think, mean that we cannot quite shunt them out of the way as mere context-setters, and get on with the rest of the play. They seem to represent two quite distinct strands of values, both of which are explored by the human experiences and actions which take place in the main part of the play. The first strand is that associated with religious piety in general – respect for sanctuary, shrine, temple. The second strand is that a city's gods are associated with the identity and ethos of the defeated community. Given the role of Poseidon (as joint founder of Troy) in straddling these two aspects, we need to ask questions about the way in which treatment meted out to the defeated is evaluated in the play as a whole.

A hint of the complexity of the issue is given in Poseidon's opening words – 'the sacred groves are deserted; the temples run with blood' (line 12). The word translated as 'deserted' (*eremos*) or 'desolate' recurs in the play (see lines 26 and 97), notably at line 603 where it is applied to the individual losing her city and at line 564 where it is used to convey the vulnerability to rape of the newly widowed lying alongside the headless bodies of their husbands. This last example of 'secular' suffering is significantly juxtaposed alongside lament about the murder of Trojans at their altars.

I want therefore to suggest that while in the opening scene Euripides is apparently primarily concerned with examples of outrage to religion, he broadens these themes in the rest of the play. He by no means shuts out the question of the treatment meted out to the defeated in general. Such evaluation does not necessarily presuppose religious criteria. Consider, for example, the pivotal role of the Greek herald Talthybius in judging, by implication, the *excess* of cruelty to the defeated enacted by his victorious compatriots. He regards slavery of Andromache and Hecabe as the inevitable result of defeat in war and the exercise of power (line 728). But he can hardly find words to convey the sacrifice of Polyxena and the killing of Astyanax (line 271 and especially lines 709–12). Through such passages, the themes of Greek and Trojan disaster are linked. The Prologue sets out the underlying theme – that the Greeks, too, face disaster and that they are themselves to blame for it. The main part of the play shows the Trojan disaster and, in exploring it, raises the further question about what exactly the Greeks are to be blamed for. Is it to be more than impiety? Do secular and religious outrages go together?

8.6 Victims and agents

I now want to turn to the other side of the coin. So far in this section, I have emphasized the role of the gods in setting the context and in explaining the action which has preceded and will follow the play. But in the play itself, they have no part in forwarding or retarding the action. The Prologue's direct relevance to the play itself is concerned with the raising of issues. However, the broader question of the direct interference of the gods in human affairs is specifically raised in the Third Episode, when Hecabe confronts Helen.

Please turn to this now (lines 860–1059) and note how each woman considers the role of the gods in human affairs in part of her argument. To what extent does Euripides present their argument as a debate about the extent of divine and human responsibility?

Discussion

Of course, the whole sequence has the anachronistic language and structure of a sophistic debate, but we will return to that aspect later. The first thing to note about Hecabe's contribution is that, although she addresses Zeus directly, she seems to be in some doubt what he represents ('inflexible law of nature or man's mind' as translated by Barlow; 'human intelligence or natural law' as translated by Vellacott, line 886). Menelaus describes such a prayer as 'strange and new', but it surely sets the parameters for the debate which is to follow, which is nominally about whether it would be unjust to put Helen to death.

Helen rests her case on attributing responsibility for the events which led to the war to humans other than herself. She includes Hecabe and Priam since they are the parents of Paris. She also blames the goddess Aphrodite, who wanted to be chosen by Paris in return for her offer of rule over Asia (line 926) and Cypris who offered Helen herself as the prize (for an artist's response to the judgement of Paris, see Illustration Booklet II.24).

In her response (lines 969ff.) Hecabe initially accepts the terms of the debate and discusses the credibility of the goddesses' conduct in human terms. But she quickly moves to the idea that the supposed stupidity of the goddesses is a mask for Helen's own intemperance and folly: 'To cloak your own guilt you dress up the gods as fools' (line 981).

The point is not that Hecabe is saying that the gods do not exist, but that she claims they do not behave in this irrational way and that such images as we have of them may be psychological projections of our own state of mind. This fits well with her later stress on the inactivity of the gods at lines 1280–1:

> Gods! Gods! Where are you? Why should I clamour to the gods?
> We called on them before, and not one heard us call.

The debate is of course a contest, an *agon*. It was traditional for the winner to be the person who spoke second. Yet in an important sense the confrontation is not a direct one. The audience is not being invited to compare like with like. Helen speaks logically, *if* her basic premises are accepted. Hecabe speaks emotionally, wanting revenge, yet her ideas derive their force from rationalist ideas about explanations of human behaviour. She does not meet Helen on the latter's terms but changes the ground, transferring the notion of responsibility from the divine to the human plane. This is what I mean by talking about tensions in Euripides' writing. ◆

In this section we have been focusing on tension between divine and secular in values and responsibilities. In the next section we will look more closely at the tension between emotion and intellect mentioned above.

Figure 35 A and B Attic red figure hydria, from Nola; the sack of Troy, by the Kleophrades painter, 490–480 (Cat.2422; ARV 189.74). This crowded band on the shoulder of a large vase shows a series of incidents from the fall of Troy. On the front of the vase (a) Priam is shown seated on an altar with his dead grandson on his lap, about to be slaughtered. On his right a Trojan woman is attacking a Greek. On the left (b) a woman is being torn from a sacred image by a warrior. This pair is usually identified as Ajax and Cassandra, and every Greek would have known her eventual fate. The images concentrate very much on the suffering. Cassandra is half-naked and defenceless, the wounds on Priam's grandson's body spout blood, and the old man clutches his head in despair. The only hopeful scenes are Aeneas stealing away with Anchises on his back, on the left (b), and the rescue of Aithra (not fully visible). What is interesting is the concentration on the sufferings of the old and the weak rather than the glorification of the Greek victory. This is a vase painted during the Persian wars when the Athenians faced the reality of the sack of their city and the possibility of slavery if they were defeated, and had parallels in Aeschylus' *Persae*. How closely do you feel this imagery matches Euripides' play? (For other representations of the Trojan Wars, see *WA* illustrations 2.11, 7.39 and 3.2–8.)

8.7 Emotion and intellect

Some critics of Euripides have described this play as a miserable tale of woe. Others have drawn on aspects such as the *agon* between Helen and Hecabe to suggest that Euripides uses the subject-matter as the framework for a series of dramatized but dry debates, drawing on sophistic models and terminology. It is certainly true that Helen and Hecabe argue by means of set rhetorical forms about the extent of Helen's responsibility for the Trojan wars. This was a conventional topic in stylized rhetoric, used by the sophist Gorgias as the basis for his *Encomium*. You will be able to study this further in Block 5. There are also other examples in the play of the use of sophistic techniques and subject-matter, for instance in Cassandra's argument about the claims of the defeated to be better off than the victors (lines 353–405). It may well be true that the convolutions of these arguments jar on the modern ear (perhaps on the ancient one too). Yet the broad issues raised about the nature of human responsibility, about what is and is not worth fighting for, are not in themselves ornamental tangents to the rest of the play. They are deeply embedded in its structure and imagery.

Please now turn to Hecabe's Monody *(lines 93–150) and re-read it, then continue to the end of the* Parodos *(line 229). As you read, look especially for the words in which the translator expresses Euripides' presentation of misery and lamentation. Then consider the impact upon the reader/audience of these words in conjunction with the status of the speakers.*

Discussion

In Hecabe's lines I would point to a combination of features. We have the vocabulary of grief and mourning, the emotional effects of which are intensified by the association with the sense of power and inevitability compressed into the sea imagery. But there is also a strong sense of the physical effects of defeat on an old woman ('lift your neck from the dust', 'outcast limits', 'prisoner and slave', 'grey hair ravaged/with the knife of mourning'). This is intensified by the greatness of her fall. She is not only an old woman but also the wife of Priam ('*shrunk* to nothing, *sunk* in mean oblivion'). One of the aspects of Euripides' writing which Aristophanes mocked was the poet's fascination with degraded royalty. However, here the impact of Hecabe's lament is derived not only from the force of the words used to describe her position – but also from the setting of her words between the cool self-assured discussion between the gods which precedes it and the lines of the Chorus which follow it. Here destruction is given a broader social context, extended to the experiences and fears of all the women of Troy. Perhaps these too are needed to 'release/Pity to match your pain' (lines 197–8), as the translator puts it. The text's original words emphasize the idea of lamentation and the translator's version is one response to the problem of dealing in English with the language associated with lament. He draws perhaps on the Aristotelian notion of tragedy as inspiring pity and fear in the audience. In any event, his translation concentrates on conveying the *effect* of the original rather than reproducing its *content*. ◆

8.8 Translation – vocabulary and feeling

Shirley Barlow has pointed out (op. cit., p.37) that the Greek language was exceptionally rich in the range of words which express the emotions of grief. (This was discussed on Cassette 1, Band 2 in relation to Prometheus.) English vocabulary is short on *modern* equivalents (the Victorians did better, but words such as 'bewail' and 'bemoan' sound odd to us now). Most of the English words now in use have a factual as well as an emotional implication – for example 'pain', 'loss', 'violence' – but we have fewer appropriate words to describe feelings. Furthermore, we lack the words to directly express what Barlow calls 'raw feelings'. The Greeks could use *aiai, pheu, e e, oimoi, io, ototoi* etc., whereas 'alas, alack, woe is me' is hopelessly stylized and faintly ludicrous in English.

Because of this, we need to bear in mind that a translated version almost certainly emphasizes the factual and instrumental element in grief at the expense of the expressive feeling.

The other way in which emotion could be directly conveyed in Greek is through poetic metre. There is a good example in the Second Episode, lines 577–607 (the lyric duet between Andromache and Hecabe). Here Euripides used two different metres and composed the dialogue of half-lines where each speaker responds in turn to the other, partly focusing on what was just said but also expressing her own concerns and emotions. In your translation, direct address to Zeus is used instead of the vocabulary of lament. Thus the impression in the original is more fragmented, perhaps more intense and certainly more personal to the characters. The broken parts of the dialogue relate rather less clearly to one another.

I suggest that at this point you re-read the whole of the Second Episode (lines 568–798) and consider how the emotional force of the broken dialogue sequence underpins and emphasizes the personal impact on the characters of the theme of the mutability of human fortune. This idea of mutability permeates the exchanges between the two women and the Athenian herald – for example, 612–15.

When you read extracts from *The Persians* in conjunction with Block 1, one of the things you noted was the way in which Aeschylus conveys the suffering of the defeated both in its own terms *and* as part of the celebration of Athenian victory. In *The Women of Troy*, Euripides is on one level apparently dealing with a historical/mythological situation, so he does not have to confront the demands of dealing *directly* with contemporary sensibilities about the war he describes. Yet, as you may have considered when reading *Antigone* in Block 2, the value of drama as a historical source is increased by the fact that it may be dealing *indirectly* with current problems. Our awareness of these problems increases when we discover how the dramatist probes sensitive issues and opens up new ones by subtle shifts of emphasis.

In *The Women of Troy* the triumph of victory is touched on but is hardly glorified, while the suffering of the defeated is portrayed as in some sense detracting from the victory – both in the sense that the Greeks are to be punished for their blasphemies and in the sense that the pain of the defeated outweighs the gain to Greek prestige achieved by the repatriation of Helen. (Was she worth it?) Euripides conveys the pain of the defeated in emotional terms since it is in the nature of defeat that the sufferers have no other means of expression. He also broadens the impact by linking the personal and the community. We saw this in the initial encounter between Hecabe and the women of Troy, but the personal and the communal are finally unified in the culminating Chorus (lines 1290ff.) in which Hecabe and the women join in hopeless lamentation. Without the emotional force and despair of the defeated, victory could remain a glorious object of aspiration, but in Euripides' play victory becomes problematic. In the next section we will turn to the nature and extent of the problems Euripides associates with this particular victory.

8.9 The world turned upside down

When the body of the child Astyanax (the name signifies ruler of the city) is being prepared for burial, Hecabe responds to the Chorus' promptings to 'intone the dirge for the dead' (lines 1227). But she goes further than this, relating this particular tragedy to the wider situation (lines 1240ff.). Her lament emphasizes two things. First, it questions the utility of sacrifices and prayers (ritual is useless for changing the course of events). Secondly, it claims that the misery and total reduction of Troy is mitigated only by the fact that the city's name will be preserved in future poetry. (This last point may strike us as odd, but it was in fact a commonplace sentiment in ancient literature.)

The lines 'heaven cast down our greatness and engulfed/All in the earth's depth' (lines 1242–3) are of particular importance, partly because they emphasize the totality of defeat but mainly because they represent the translator's response to the way in which the Greek text pivots on the sense to be given to the words 'overthrown' or 'overturn'. Reversal of fortune, the fall of the great, is another commonplace theme in Greek tragedy, but in this play Euripides elaborates the idea of *fall* to explore the implications of *reversal*. An alternative translation follows the original text more closely and clarifies the point:

> So the gods amounted to nothing after all!
> There was only my suffering and their discriminating hatred of Troy.
> My sacrifices were useless.
> And yet had not God turned the world upside down, we should have acquired no significance, and should have remained unsung, instead of giving themes of song for future generations.

(tr. Barlow, op. cit.)

In our translation the phrase 'the world turned upside down' is used at line 614 by Andromache to express the total reversal of her situation, the descent from royalty to slavery.

So, next, we shall look at some of the different ways in which Euripides explores this idea of reversal, of turning upside down. I shall begin by looking at the way Euripides exploits this with reference to the *situation* of the characters and the shape of the *action*, and move from this to looking at his use of *images* and *epithets* as a means of transferring the traditional conventions of reference, and thus suggesting fragmentation in the accepted norms of social order and values.

8.10 Reversal in situation and action

We are accustomed in Western literature to the tragic tradition in which the protagonist's fall from apparent heights of pride and prosperity is depicted and analysed (Oedipus, for example, or King Lear). According to many interpreters of Aristotle, this 'fall' is the result of some tragic flaw in character or judgement. Euripides does not use this perspective in his play: he uses the theme of 'fall' in a way which is both more flexible and more structural.

Jot down the names of those characters who 'fall' from their high positions in the course of the play. Then consider what it is about this aspect of the play that a mere listing of characters leaves out.

Discussion _____

I listed:

Hecabe → queen, wife of Priam → widow → slave

Cassandra → princess/priestess, daughter of Priam → concubine

Andromache → wife of Hector → widow → concubine

    " → mother of Astyanax → childless

Astyanax → son of Hector → killed (*literally* cast down)

Chorus of women of Troy → wives and mothers in prosperous city

→ slavery.

It is difficult to decide about *Helen*. From being the partner of Paris she is reclaimed by Menelaus and seems to face death, but we know (as did the Greek audience) that she in fact prospered. Helen's survival was a basic feature of the myth and hence not subject to change by the dramatist.

Talthybius and Menelaus as victorious Greeks clearly do not fall in the course of the play, yet we know from previous knowledge of the myth, from the Prologue and from Cassandra's prophecy (lines 429ff.) that the victors are to be beset by disaster on the voyage home. That ironic dimension is part of the framework within which we interpret what happens in the play.

A mere list of the fate of individual characters also leaves out the dominating effect of the idea of Troy itself as an entity. It not only represents the focal loyalties and gods of a collection of people. It was an identifiable place, it had *earth* ('the earth you loved...', line 1318). The fall of the female members of the ruling house also involves for them a change of location. Thus 'situation' implies not only one's place in the hierarchy, it refers to *where* one is, literally. ◆

8.11 Situation and image

Images such as ships, walls, tower, fire permeate the text, giving a poetic unity to the external impact of the action and the inner experiences of the characters. The use of ship images is a prime example, but be aware of the others too as you work on the text.

On a simple level the Greek ships are the means by which the change in the situation of the Trojans is effected. The physical presence of the ships frames the action. At the beginning Hecabe's *monody*, permeated with the imagery of the sea and ships, takes in both the role of the ships in the action of the play (Strophe 2) and the metaphorical expression of the impact of defeat (Strophe 1, '*shrunk*', '*sunk*'; Antistrophe I, 'restless rocking'). At the beginning of the Fourth Episode, Andromache's final cries are on Neoptolemus' ship as it leaves harbour (lines 1160–1). The final words of the play, 'Ships of Greece, we come!', reflect the finality in Trojan terms of this reversal of situation. The ships are central to the play not only as the physical instruments of change but as images of the personal suffering of the characters.

The importance of geographical place as well as social status in determining 'situation' has significant repercussions in Euripides' suggestion of ambiguity in values in the play. The suffering of the Trojan women is epitomized in their loss of their homes and hearths, the place where they belong, the place where it is appropriate for them to be. Exile involves a loss of identity. The corollary is that it is the Trojans who may be said to have died nobly in defence of their gods, their earth, their homes and hearths. The lines in which Cassandra celebrates this, read almost like a critical commentary on the values expressed in the Funeral Speech in Thucydides:

> ... the men of Troy, whose glory it was
> To die defending their own country! Those who fell
> Were carried back by comrades to their homes, prepared
> For burial by the hands they loved, and laid to rest
> In the land that bore them.

(lines 386–90)

Conversely, it is the Greeks who have left their country, to die far from home, buried not by their own families but in 'alien earth' (line 380). 'What did they die for? To thrust invasion from their borders/Or siege from their town walls?' (lines 376–7). There seems to be a sense in which being taken from their native soil cuts off both Greeks and Trojans from their proper place within their own framework of social and moral values.

8.12 Image and epithet

Euripides makes Cassandra present this reversal in values through a series of word pictures ('I will *show* you', line 366) which have the effect of focusing the audience's attention on the symmetry between the expressed values of the Trojans and their actions (although they are defeated) and the violent disjunction between the values and actions of the Greeks (although they are victorious). The lines come at a point of calm reflection for Cassandra following the madness of the 'wedding aria'. Her depiction of Greeks and Trojans inverts the value of victory and defeat and she is presented as, in a sense, standing outside her own madness – 'this at least is truth untouched with madness' (lines 374–5). Yet the effect of the reflective sequence depends on its relationship with the scene preceding it.

Please now re-read lines 292–404. To what extent in lines 306–364 could it be said that 'the world is upside down'?

Discussion

The opening lines represent a dramatic expression of the dislocation in Cassandra's mind. Defeated and captive, she celebrates with torches. She celebrates her wedding, but in reality is to be a concubine and should have remained a virgin (the language used suggests marriage with religious observance, which strengthens the contrast). That which her mother laments is for her a cause of celebration. This mis-match of ceremony and degradation is, for the Chorus, a sign of Cassandra's madness. To Hecabe it amounts to sacrilege.

Then in the space of a few lines (353–364) Euripides moves from this dramatic exploration of the frenzy of mismatch between Cassandra's real situation and the value she places on it towards a different key in which she is impelled to show and comment on the wider contrast between the values asserted in apparent victory and apparent defeat. Her madness made the onlookers say, 'she does not understand the meaning of marriage and slavery'. The reflective passage questions the validity of victory achieved in an alien environment. This reversal in perspective too is rejected by the Chorus. (It was Cassandra's fate to foretell the truth and not be believed.)

Both sequences, from very different perspectives, threaten our sense of certainty about what has happened. When Cassandra says she will come 'triumphant to the house of death', she is referring to her presence at Agamemnon's murder of Klytemnestra. The word used, *nikephoros* (victory-bringing), is usually applied to male heroes. Thus in one sense it is inappropriate for any woman, still less a captive concubine. In another sense it makes us re-examine our assumptions about what we are to understand by victory and by the heroic. Cassandra's function as 'truth-teller' was another basic element in the myth. It therefore gives her 'madness' a special status which can be exploited by the dramatist, secure in the knowledge that her utterances are likely to be significant. (We might compare Aeschylus' portrayal of Cassandra in the *Agamemnon*.) ◆

I have concentrated on Cassandra's *monody* because it brings together dramatically those elements of situation, image and language through which we are approaching the theme of reversal. It is also structurally pivotal in the play's questioning of assumed values and is an important counterpart to Andromache's role in the Second Episode which we shall be considering later. But as you work on the play you might like to look for further examples of unexpected use or even transfer of epithet. For example, look at line 1021 in Episode Three when Helen is accused of wanting the Phrygians to 'kneel' before her. Prostration was in fact a non-Greek custom. As the original Greek makes clear, Helen is in fact behaving like a barbarian. Elsewhere the epithet 'barbarian' is directly transferred on to the Greeks, notably in Andromache's outburst, line 766, 'Hellenes! Inventors of barbaric cruelties!'

To complete your work on this section, please now re-read the Fourth Episode, lines 1123–end. As you read, consider how Euripides elaborates the theme of reversal; in what ways is the world 'upside down'?

Discussion ————————————————————————————

We have already dealt with the change in geographical and social situation for the women of the defeated. To this we can add a reversal in the natural order of things. Andromache is parted from her child and exiled. The child has been killed by the Greeks. The child is buried on his father's shield instead of in a coffin. He is given a warrior's burial in his native soil although he was not old enough to experience battle.

The actual burial of the child contains elements of conscious role-reversal, commented on by Hecabe. He is buried and lamented by his grandmother, not the reverse (lines 1181ff.). He wears for the burial the kind of splendid garment he should have worn for his wedding. Less straightforwardly, the use of the shield for burial combines inappropriateness for a child's funeral with symbolic association with Hector.

The violent overturning of values implicit in this role reversal is elaborated in Hecabe's bitter epitaph:

> ... What would a poet write for you
> As epitaph? 'This child the Argives killed because
> They feared him.' An inscription to make Hellas blush.

> (lines 1188–90)

The point is taken up in Hecabe's description of the victorious Greeks, 'shaking with fear ... cowards' (1165–6). It is not just the world of the Trojans which is turned upside down. (It is interesting that Hecabe's is a generalized verdict on the Greeks. We might consider the extent to which it is mitigated by the conduct of Talthybius and Neoptolemus.) The killing of the child and his burial on the shield provides the dramatic climax to the play, representing the end of Troy and the drawing together of the themes of defeat and reversal. It can be (and doubtless was) played out for its pathos. One lingering doubt remains. In associating the child with the shield of his father and the reversal of his hopes, Hecabe symbolically buries Hector's image with the shield. It is precisely those associations which led the Greeks to ensure no male heir remained. As so often when we try to pin him down to a fixed perspective, Euripides eludes us. The more he emphasizes the pathos, the more he demonstrates the necessity of the killing, from the Greeks' point of view. ◆

In the next section we will try in an different way to see if we can reconcile explorations and conclusions in the play.

8.13   The centrality of the female characters

The mere fact that female characters are at the centre of the action and experiences of a Greek tragedy is far from unusual: we can cite the dominant role of Klytemnestra in the *Agamemnon* of Aeschylus, of Antigone in Sophocles' play, and of Medea in another play by Euripides. But all these plays have female protagonists who in some sense initiate the action. These protagonists tend to be presented in the play as 'honorary men' because of the vigour of their actions and/or are the objects of misogynistic comments from other characters or the chorus, who draw attention to the dangerous characteristics associated with females. This is not so in *The Women of Troy*. Here Helen is only in a limited sense the occasion for the war. She is not a prime mover in the play itself nor one of the dominant characters. In the other plays mentioned above, the leading female is in a role of direct conflict or competition with a dominant male individual. Again, this is not so in *The Women of Troy* where the women are passive victims of a situation rather than in conflict with one individual male. Even the Menelaus/Helen confrontation is translated into an *agon* between Helen and Hecabe, although significantly this *agon* then to some extent gives the women 'male' debating stances and arguments. Against this we can set the fact that it is the suffering and emotions of the females which demand our attention. The male characters are foils in the major episodes. Therefore, in this section, I want to consider the implications of the paradox that the female characters are both *central* and *passive*, and to approach questions about how the dramatist's presentation of the female characters reveals assumptions and uncertainties about the way in which women were perceived. To what extent would we be justified in claiming that Euripides' presentation questions the conventions of the time?

I am going to accept without arguing it through in detail that Helen is not intended to be regarded as a 'woman of Troy', nor to be included among the sufferers. However, the terms of the *agon* in the Third Episode are germane to our discussion here (see Section 8.6 above). The rhetorical debate between Helen and Hecabe is concerned with the question of *blame*. Once the focus on responsibility shifts from the gods to human beings, two accusations can be made. One is that Hecabe is to blame for allowing Paris to live. The second is that Helen is to blame, not only for coming to Troy and remaining there alive, but also in a more general sense for the power of female sexuality. Yet the debate seems more important for its role in transferring responsibility from divine to secular than for an attempt to make the precise nature of Helen's responsibility a central issue. If we allow that Hecabe has the final word, her command to Menelaus:

> Kill Helen and establish in all lands this law,
> That every wife unfaithful to her husband dies.

> (lines 1030–1)

takes on a chill irony, since we know both that Helen will not be killed and that it is precisely Andromache's possession of the qualities Helen lacks which governs her fate among the Greeks. (Look especially at lines 644ff., another ironic comment on the attitude to women's behaviour expressed in the Funeral Speech in Thucydides and the Catch-22 situation in which the female virtues place the woman who is captured by a man not her husband.)

The focus, then, is on the undeserved suffering of the central female characters – Hecabe, Cassandra, Andromache and the chorus of Trojan women. Not only is their suffering undeserved in the sense that is does not involve a personalized or social retribution for wrong-doing; it is also *unchosen* (contrast Antigone or Prometheus). Thus we need to ask for what end female suffering is exploited by Euripides.

The first point that has to be made is that the kind of suffering inflicted is specific to females (and children). Men who are defeated in battle die, women are enslaved (compare Thucydides 5.116). Their suffering is both permanent and total. Euripides gives us images of the physical suffering but it is the mental anguish which he explores. We saw earlier that Euripides includes both direct expression of misery in lament and the psychological disarray of the anguished mind. He thus builds onto the conventional/expected role of the women to mourn and lament, an appreciation of the personal and human impact of material and psychological destitution. This is worked through successively in the solos of Hecabe, Cassandra and Andromache. (It would be worth studying in detail how each moves through lament to revelation of the psychology of suffering.)

The second and related point is that, although he gives the female characters a personal and psychological status, his starting point is their relationship to the defeated males. My outline chart in Section 8.10 above set this out. Hecabe is the *widow* of Priam, Andromache *widow* of Hector, *mother* of Astyanax, Cassandra is *daughter* of Priam, the women of Troy are the *mothers*, *wives* and *daughters* of the defeated. If the males are defeated in battle, this is what happens to their dependants, and we know from Herodotus and Thucydides that this was as least as true in the fifth century as in Homeric epic. Nowhere in the play does Euripides (so far as I can see) question the conventional relationship between male and female in society. He assumes that in a military context women will be objects of male sexual aggression and, with other parts of the *oikos*, expropriated by the victors. What he does do, however, is convey the impact of this on the people concerned *and* by treating in tandem the effects of blasphemous outrage and personal outrage suggest that the effects may be analogous, whichever the cause. (I think we should not underestimate the originality of his treatment of suffering from the *viewpoint* of the women concerned.) Also, he uses the female characters to challenge the *sense* of the heroic tradition in competition and warfare – an example is in Cassandra's reflections at lines 372ff., where she points out how the Greeks have, in coming to Troy, actually destroyed at home those values they claim to preserve. Therefore we might conclude that, while Euripides does not radically challenge the conventional values attached to the place of women in the *oikos*, he does, in giving them psychological and reflective status (in contrast to Pericles in Thucydides 2.46), use them as a means for questioning the congruence between expressed values and actions in society. (I will return in the concluding section to the problem of how far, in questioning the relation of values to actions in heroic society, Euripides is also questioning these relationships in his own society.)

At this point, I suggest that you re-read the Second Episode (Hecabe and Andromache), lines 565–796, and consider the extent to which Euripides is paradoxically assuming a framework of certain values and questioning their sense.

8.14   Afterword

I said at the beginning of your work on *The Women of Troy* that our treatment of it would be limited and would concentrate on opening up certain questions which you will need to consider in other contexts in the next part of the course. Here, I am going to try to summarize briefly what I take to be the main issues, and I hope you will add your own, both before and after you work on Block 5.

1   In the course of the play, Euripides probes the use of concepts such as 'victory' and 'barbarian', especially by examining the relationship between a fact or action and the value placed on it. He does this by using dramatic and literary technique. In Block 5 you will be studying the method of systematic questioning used by Socrates to approach similar problems. You might also compare Euripides' treatment of these problems with Thucydides' claim (Book 3.82; see also Block 3, Section 9) that political crisis towards the end of the Peloponnesian War was accompanied by moral crisis, and that established concepts came to be (mis)applied to new situations, thus fragmenting the accepted pattern of language use.

2   Euripides examines the relationship between divine and secular. In particular he gives a voice to scepticism about the utility of religious ritual and propitiation. (NB This scepticism is not the same as atheism. Denying that gods respond to human approaches is not the same as denying their existence.) He also opens up the question of what we are to understand by piety and blasphemy. (This is closely related to (1) above, and is a topic you will be studying in depth in Block 5.) In the play Euripides juxtaposes examples of impiety (and consequent punishment for the Greeks) with secular outrages, which are not punished but cause a level of human suffering which he feels it necessary to explore. What are we to make of this dual perspective? The other main way in which he examines the relation between divine and secular is by re-focusing the question of the moral responsibility held by humans.

You will be able to take these points further in the next block. The fact that they are raised by Euripides suggests a substantial degree of religious tolerance (but contrast the Herms and Mysteries incidents, see Section 7). One of the questions raised by Blocks 4 and 5 concerns the extent to which this tolerance was threatened by the stress of revolution and defeat in war at the end of the century.

3   Euripides also raises the question of the relationship between the values of his society and the past. He takes an incident from the heroic and mythological past but, in selecting and adapting the basic subject-matter, he re-focuses it on areas of contemporary concern. You have seen detailed examples in the text of references to, and comment on, the ideology of his own time. I said earlier that a re-examination of the relationship of divine and secular does not make this an atheistic play; equally an examination from a new angle of the effects of war does not make it a pacifist play – the important contrast is rather between the moral effects of waging a defensive war at home and carrying out an aggressive campaign abroad. Euripides is asking whether there *can* be moral constraints on the way war is waged. Implicitly Euripides finds heroic values wanting because they jar in the context of the *civic* values which he illustrates and discusses through his female characters.

Equally, the fact that the females are instrumental in opening up this debate and that their suffering is given an independent psychological status, does not necessarily make this a 'feminist' play. Euripides is writing within an accepted framework of values concerning the role and social status of women. You will need to consider how far, if at all, he questions that framework. We noticed that, in the *agon* between Helen and Hecabe, Euripides makes the women use the language and attitudes of masculine debate. Elsewhere in the play, do the female characters react to their suffering in terms which are determined by the conventions of their gender and role? Or is there any sign of an independent female voice with its own language and attitudes? (If this interests you, compare Cassandra's speech 353–404 with her departing lines 423–461.)

While reading an earlier draft of this block, Sir Kenneth Dover commented to me that:

> the Greeks tended to regard war as being just as inevitable a part of life as bad weather. Awareness of the suffering inflicted by war did not necessarily lead them to think that it was wrong to inflict such suffering by waging war; equally, acceptance of war as part of life did not diminish their awareness of suffering.

That said, just as Euripides has selected and adapted from the heroic past of Greece in terms of the perspectives of his own times, so modern versions take inspiration from those aspects of the Athenian drama which strike chords in our own experience. You might like to look back at the TV Notes for TV1 and 2 and consider how you would approach authentic and realistic productions or experimental versions of *The Women of Troy*.

J.P. Vernant has written: 'tragedy is a debate with a past that is still alive'. Clearly Euripides is debating with the heroic tradition of individual competition, but in tension with the examination of collective values, which is of equal importance in the play. How far is he extending the debate to the inherited civic and military values of his own *polis*? TV3 explored some aspects of the relationship between the theatre and the state. If you want to think further about this, compare your notes on Cassette Lecture 3 which examines some aspects of the civic ritual binding the individual and the *polis*. Refer back to Section 6 on the derivation of civic, military and social values from heroic models, and especially think about the values expressed in the debate preceding the invasion of Sicily (Thucydides 6.8–26). You may like to return to this question after you have worked on Block 5. In assessing the extent to which *The Women of Troy* helps us assess tension and change in fifth-century attitudes, remember that the trilogy of which it is a part did not win!

8.15 Further Reading

I hope many of you will want to read more Euripides. *The Bacchae* is studied in the next block. It would be especially useful to read *Medea* first (available in translation in Penguin).

Euripides: Trojan Women (with introduction, translation and commentary by Shirley A. Barlow), Aris and Phillips, 1986. (The edition also contains a general introduction to the ancient theatre, to Greek Tragedy and to Euripides.) I warmly acknowledge the contribution of this volume to suggesting ideas and themes for studying in this block.

BARLOW, S.A. (1971) 'The imagery of Euripides' (Methuen, 1971), Chapter 10.5 in EASTERLING, P.E. and KNOX, B.M.W. (eds) (1985) *Greek Literature*, Cambridge University Press (The Cambridge History of Classical Literature Vol.I).

CROALLY, N.T. (1994) *Euripidean Polemic: the Trojan Women and the function of tragedy*, Cambridge University Press.

VERNANT, J.P. and VIDAL-NAQUET, P. (1981) *Tragedy and Myth in Ancient Greece* (English translation by Janet Lloyd, 1981), Harvester Press.

CONCLUSION TO THE BLOCK

During the weeks you have spent on this block, you have been working on a very wide range of source material and have been asked to begin to relate to some fairly demanding ideas about how we can analyse Athenian society, its attitudes, assumptions and debates.

It is worth emphasizing that we do not expect you to have thought through in detail every suggestion we have made. Integration between the themes and topics we have studied is a continuing and developing process. You will be spending more time on it during the Revision Block (Block 6). However, a checklist of what you should have achieved at this stage may be helpful.

1   *Sources*
    You should have studied carefully the major written texts and examples of art and architecture included in the block.

2   *Methods*
    You should have practised and thought about the methods of analysing the different types of evidence and be familiar with the approaches taught in the audio-cassettes. Especially relevant are:

    Cassette 2, Band 1 for inscriptions.

    Cassette 2, Band 3 for 'Gaps in the evidence' and study of the mental approaches of the Athenians.

    Cassette 3, Band 1 for the use of evidence from comedy.

    Cassette 3, Bands 2 and 3 for analysing evidence from art and architecture.

    Cassette 3, Band 4 for approaching *The Women of Troy* as a dramatic work.

3   *Relation to the overall theme of tension and change*
    You should have begun to think about how you can *use* in a broader context the evidence you have studied, either by using the guiding questions suggested in the block or by developing a strategy of your own.

Before you go further, look back to Section 1.2 in the introduction to this block, and think about how the evidence we have studied fits in with or 'straddles' the categories of analysis I summarized there.

Notice especially that the evidence we have considered in this block relates to the interface between environment, way of life, beliefs and attitudes. We have been concerned with *how* the Athenians lived and *why*, and the ways in which they thought about or debated the practical issues concerned with the community. What we did not do to any great extent was to consider the assumptions about the nature of the universe (and the place of human beings in it) as well as the nature of judgements and language which underlie debate about community and political issues.

In the next block, Chris Emlyn-Jones will identify some of these philosophical and religious assumptions and consider the extent to which they too were challenged during the fifth century. Thus Block 5 also contributes to study of the 'tensions and change' theme with which we have begun to engage in this block.

Figure credits

Courtesy of Museum of Fine Arts, Boston, H.L. Pierce Fund: *Figure 1.*

Reproduced from Louis Dupré, *Voyage Athènes et Constantinople*, 1825, Paris, photograph by courtesy of Cambridge University Library: *Figure 2.*

Reproduced from R. Atkinson and H. Bagenel (1926) *Theory and Elements of Architecture*, London, Benn, vol.1, fig.19: *Figure 3.*

Bibliothèque Nationale, Paris: *Figure 7.*

Reproduced by permission of Professor Dr E. Beger and Antikenmuseum Basel: *Figures 8 and 9.*

Reproduced by courtesy of Professor H.F. Mussche and Comité des Fouilles Belges en Grèce: *Figure 10.*

Antikenmuseum Staatliche Museen Preussischer Kulturbesitz Berlin (West), photo – Ingrid Geske-Heiden: *Figure 11.*

American School of Classical Studies at Athens, Agora Excavations: *Figures 12 and 30.*

Plans and drawings by John Ellis Jones, from 'Town and country houses of Attica in Classical times', *Miscellanea Graeca 1, Thorikos and Laurion in Archaic and Classical Times*, 1975, University of Ghent, by permission of John Ellis Jones, Professor H.F. Mussche and Comité des Fouilles Belges en Grèce: *Figures 13, 15, 16, 19, 20 and 22–5.*

Reproduced from David Moore Robinson, *Excavations at Olynthus XII*, 1946, by permission of the publishers, Johns Hopkins University Press, Baltimore: *Figure 14.*

Plan by John Travlos, 1962, reproduced by permission of the American School of Classical Studies at Athens, Agora Excavations: *Figure 17.*

Plan by W.B. Dinsmoor Jr, 1971, reproduced by permission of the American School of Classical Studies at Athens, Agora Excavations: *Figure 18.*

Reproduced from *Thorikos: La vie dans une ville minière de la Grèce antique*, 1986, Brussels, 'De Tinne Pot', by permission of Kredietbank, Professor H.F. Mussche and Comité des Fouilles Belges en Grèce: *Figure 21.*

Antikenmuseum Staatliche Museen Preussischer Kulturbesitz Berlin (West), photo – Ute Jung: *Figure 26.*

Reproduced by permission of the Trustees of the British Museum: *Figure 27.*

Ashmolean Museum, Oxford: *Figures 28 and 29.*

Mansell collection: *Figures 30 and 33.*

Department of Near-Eastern and Classical Antiquities, National Museum, Copenhagen: *Figure 31.*

Reconstruction by John Travlos, reproduced by permission of the American School of Classical Studies at Athens, Agora Excavations: *Figure 32.*

Musée des Beaux-Arts, Lyons: *Figure 34.*

Deutschen Archaologischen Institut, Rome: *Figure 35.*